Against
the Clock

The incredible story of the 7/49

Ron Ayres

Whitehorse Press
North Conway, New Hampshire

Front and back cover photographs are by Dennis
Robinson.

Unless otherwise noted, all other photographs are by
the author.

You may contact the author through the Internet at:
    ron@ronayres.com

We recognize that some words, model names, and
designations mentioned herein are the property of the
trademark holder. We use them for identification
purposes only.

An Incredible Journeys Book
Published August 1999 by
    Whitehorse Press
    P.O. Box 60
    North Conway, New Hampshire 03860 USA
    Phone: 603-356-6556 or 800-531-1133
    Fax: 603-356-6590
    E-mail: CustomerService@WhitehorsePress.com
    Internet: www.WhitehorsePress.com

Whitehorse Press is a trademark of Kennedy
Associates.

ISBN 1-884313-19-1

5 4 3 2 1

Printed in the United States of America

Dedication

To my wife, Barbara Robinson—
The greatest sidekick a man could hope to have.

Contents

Foreword

On Riding at Sunrise

"The headlight cuts a small swath, a tight tunnel through the swirling nothingness of night. Riding through this blackness, suspended but for two wheels, the long distance rider is once again alone with his private thoughts, again alone with his fears.

Imagined fears. Real fears.

Then, in darkened sky just ahead to the east, the rider sees it—no, too strong a word—he senses it once again.

A faint pale wispiness of glow.

Not on the horizon, but higher still. As if some yet unseen city lies far distant, its light perhaps making an inverse of mirage. A dark band of night still envelops that terminator of land and sky as the emptiness of night wraps 'round the rider and his swift moving mount. With this emptiness now his sole companion, the aching void is somehow strange comfort.

But not even a slight glimmer is this first ephemeral light.

Dawn's early light.

An ancient, unspoken, unwritten promise is to be fulfilled once again.

A reaffirmation, another beginning will unfold before the rider. His forward pace remains unchanged. Headlong to partake, to commune, glad to accept the oncoming challenge, he continues forward, relishing this purity, this special sanctity, this magic time of The Ride.

A sweet rhythm of Nature beats out before and through him at its unchanged, unhurried pace. Unflappable, intractable, the cycle of sunlight now again plays at its own fixed tempo, its own measure and rate. The rider's progress does not diminish as the heavenly glow becomes a ruddy red, the horizon still strangely darker than the brightening sky just overhead.

A new day waits to be molded just across this looming, still-blank horizon.

A day rich, pregnant, now at the cusp. A new day to be first born once again, fertile with opportunity unbound. The bright, orange rays, then the hot, golden orb, now the blinding, white flash silently scream its arrival.

It dawns empty, starkly barren, blank but fresh. This new day.

It waits to be filled, populated, colored, and completely used.

A new mural will be painted across it from the rider's palette of experience yet unknown. A tableau unlike all before.

The rider presses on, darkness conquered. He presses on into this new-found day.

For the sun has again risen.

He rides on.

He rides on to embrace what is yet to be."

—*Warren Harhay*

Acknowledgments

I began writing this book to chronicle my record ride. I soon realized the story is about something more meaningful and inspiring than a lone motorcyclist visiting 49 states in a week. It's really about the motorcycle endurance riding community and the incredible bond existing between these ardent enthusiasts.

I'm extremely grateful for the enthusiastic support of the more than 200 friends who volunteered at 49 checkpoints to provide encouragement and validate the ride. As I worked on this book, I was reminded of the personal sacrifices and the commitment of time that so many friends so willingly made to help me. I was impressed not only with their dedication, but also the creativity they demonstrated in coming up with solutions to potential problems. I'm incredibly fortunate to have friends such as these.

I'm also grateful to my wife Barbara, my son Brad, and to my sister-in-law Roberta Robinson for their round-the-clock efforts to keep the riding community informed of my progress and to coordinate checkpoint activities.

1
The Velcro Award

I'm horrified!

The pocket of my riding suit is open and my bag of receipts is gone. I'm so stunned at the discovery that my gloom is visible to the service station clerk. She asks what's wrong.

"Nothing," I mutter. For a moment, I'm too stunned to walk away.

"Thank you," I murmur quietly, as I walk to the door. I feel depression and embarrassment at the same time.

I walk to the motorcycle and lean against it for several minutes because I can't think of anything else to do. I glance toward the attendant and see her glancing at me, obviously curious.

I'd been collecting the receipts to prove that I'd visited the previous 42 states as I attempted to break a record for visiting all 48 contiguous states. I hadn't placed the receipts anywhere except in the pocket of the riding suit since I began the ride in Denver, less than five nights ago. I'm certain they aren't packed on the motorcycle. Anger and disgust rise to join my feelings of depression and embarrassment. I perform a perfunctory search of the bike, knowing I won't find the receipts. They have been lost, or left behind.

My dilemma is all the more disgraceful as this is the *second* time within a year that I've lost paperwork during a major endurance rally, after investing several days, as many sleepless nights, and thousands of miles in the ride. I recall how I lost 600 points during the 1995 Iron Butt Rally when my collection of receipts blew out of my tank bag somewhere between Abilene and Fort Worth.

I think of the embarrassment that I'll experience when I return to rally headquarters in Denver and admit that, once again, I've lost my paperwork. Denver was the starting and ending location of the 8/48, so named because the participants were attempting to travel through all 48 states in eight days. I not only hoped to successfully complete the rally, I intended to use it as a vehicle to challenge the existing 48-state record. Instead, at the celebration dinner after the event, Rallymaster Steve Chalmers presented me with a special "Velcro" award:

> *Presented to Ron Ayres by The Motorcycle Endurance Rider Association For His Uncanny Ability To Snatch Defeat From The Jaws of Victory By Losing His Paperwork In Two Different Rallies.*

Thus ended my ignominious first attempt at breaking the 48-state record.

2

The 48-State Quest

The idea of visiting the 48 contiguous states in the shortest possible time has attracted the attention of serious endurance motorcyclists for years. In 1986, Jeff Brody, a director of the BMW Owners Association, claimed to have ridden to the 48 contiguous states in eleven days, seven hours, and fifteen minutes. The claim inspired Bob Higdon, known widely in the BMW motorcycle community for his riding and writing, to try to beat his record. Bob's first attempt was unsuccessful. He attributed his failure, at least in part, to discomfort caused by the model motorcycle he had selected. He replaced the motorcycle and attacked the record again in August, 1987. This ride was successful, and was documented with a time of ten days, twenty-one hours, and thirty-seven minutes.

Mike Kneebone, president of the Iron Butt Association, had wanted to do a 48-state ride for many years and began his planning long before Higdon's ride. Mike and Fran Crane, a well-known female endurance rider, tackled the record together. Although best friends now, Higdon and Kneebone had not yet met. Neither knew of the others' plans.

In 1988, Fran and Mike established a Guinness record after they visited 48 states in six days, thirteen hours, and twenty-one minutes. Their route started in Pendleton, Oregon, and ended in Brattleboro, Vermont, and covered 7,703 miles. Higdon's route began and ended in Washington, D.C., but required traveling more than 8,400 miles.

Fran Crane and Mike Kneebone pose in 1988 before their own
record-breaking ride

These were all individual attempts. In 1996, Steve
Chalmers conducted the first official 48-state rally, the 8/48.
The format was straightforward. Riders left Denver at midnight on Friday, August 30th, and had eight days to visit all 48
contiguous states, collecting receipts as proof, before returning
to Denver for a celebration banquet.

Since first learning of the 48-state record, I became in-
trigued with breaking it. I assumed that Chalmers' 8/48 Rally
could provide the format for doing so. I could participate in the
rally and attempt to break the 48-state record at the same time.

As I reviewed the requirements to qualify for a Guinness record, however, I identified several obstacles. First, the 8/48
would begin and end in Denver, requiring a longer ride than if I
could select different starting and ending locations. Although I
discussed this concern with Chalmers, he wasn't receptive to
changing the starting and ending points to accommodate my
desire to break a Guinness record.

There were other obstacles. The rules for the Guinness record were more complex than for the 8/48. First, two witnesses
in each state would have to sign a form validating my visit. The

Guinness organization would then send copies of the forms to the witnesses for verification after the rally. If a witness didn't confirm that the forms were valid, the stop wouldn't count and my time spent on the attempt would be wasted. Naturally, I was concerned about being able to find reliable witnesses at all of the stops. Second, the Guinness record would have to be made without the benefit of the auxiliary fuel capacity allowed for the 8/48. I had already equipped my motorcycle with an auxiliary fuel tank and thought I needed it to be competitive in the 8/48. Deciding I wasn't prepared for a proper assault on the Guinness record, I opted to go for the 8/48 win and save the Guinness record for another occasion.

After the 8/48, Chalmers asked me to write an article for the MERA (Motorcycle Endurance Rider Association) web site. As I began writing the article, the disappointment that accompanied my Velcro blunder returned. I set the article aside and studied the Velcro Award that I had framed and hung on the wall of my den. I knew if I didn't beat the existing 48-state record it would be a great disappointment in my life. I resolved to beat the existing record *and* set a new record *category* at the same time, and I used the article as the vehicle to announce my plan. I established a goal of visiting the 48 contiguous states in less than six days. Following that, I'd continue to Alaska to set a record for visiting the 49 North American states in less than one week. I dubbed the project the "7/49."

After my well-publicized documentation fiasco, I was determined to plan my 7/49 attempt to insure its success. There was nothing I could do to protect myself completely from mechanical failure or an accident, but I was determined to plan so thoroughly that I would virtually eliminate the possibility of personal failure.

3

Obsession

My sister-in-law says that I'm the only person she knows who could be crouching in a ditch during a dangerous hailstorm, happy as a frog, fantasizing about how great it would be to be floating on a small boat in the middle of the ocean during a hurricane. She offered this hyperbole to illustrate what she believes is my strange compulsion to deprive myself of comfort, shelter, sleep, and all other semblance of normal life while riding a motorcycle to the limits of human endurance. She thinks that even among the most zealous motorcyclists, I am unique.

She's wrong, however. I have several hundred friends who share my compulsion for endurance riding.

We're frequently asked why riders participate in endurance events. What motivates us to ride so many miles in a day? What do we think about for all those hours? Isn't it totally boring? The implication is that being forced to be alone with one's thoughts for so long would be unpleasant.

To answer the "why" question, it's necessary to first answer another question that's asked frequently: the "how" question. How can you *possibly* be comfortable after riding several hundred miles? Isn't it dangerous to ride a motorcycle when you're so exhausted? This is often accompanied by a reference to how uncomfortable it would be to ride so far in a car, suggesting that riding those distances in a car should be more comfortable than doing so on a motorcycle. For me, the opposite is true. I wouldn't be nearly as comfortable after riding 1,000 miles in a car as I am on a motorcycle.

To ride such distances safely, endurance riders must be able to avoid debilitating fatigue, and to do that, they must be able to stay relatively comfortable. Comfortable distance riding requires equipment, clothing, and accessories not generally used by most motorcyclists. I couldn't comfortably ride 1,000 miles in one day on most stock motorcycles. But equipped with a suitable seat and other optional equipment, I can do it repetitively. Other necessities include a waterproof riding suit, boots and gloves, a good full-face helmet, earplugs, high intensity driving lights, heated hand grips (or electric gloves), a throttle lock, and a drinking system. For cold weather, I also use an electrically-heated vest and chaps.

Although it isn't necessary for endurance riders to maintain an athlete's physique, physical conditioning and good eating habits are helpful. It's important to develop the muscles that are employed during long rides, and that's best done by riding long distances regularly. No rider should expect to be able to ride multiple 1,000-mile days on the first attempt.

Given that it's possible to ride so far in relative comfort, *why* do we do it?

I can only tell you why I do it, although I think my fellow riders share similar feelings. Simply stated, I love riding so much that I don't like to stop. Endurance riding makes me feel young, adventuresome, and totally unrestrained. Before a "high intensity" ride of several days or more, I feel like a child waiting for Christmas. And actually riding the distance is like having an infinite supply of presents that I never tire of opening.

Some of the most enjoyable times I've spent on a motorcycle have been touring leisurely with my wife Barbara on the pillion. But the experience is totally different than when I ride alone for days on end with minimal interruptions for eating and sleeping. Like most endurance riders, I prefer to ride alone because I don't like to complicate the ride by having to match fuel, eating, and rest requirements with other riders.

Shortly after beginning a long ride, a rhythm sets in and I enter a state of well being and ecstasy that can best be described as a trance. That doesn't mean I'm inattentive to what is happening around me. I've become accustomed to consciously observing traffic, road conditions, and potential animal appearances. The ability to remain attentive and avoid accidents is as much a sign of professional endurance riding as being able to handle a motorcycle competently. I welcome the demand for responsibility; it's part of the cost of entry to be able to participate in the sport safely. Except in the relatively few instances in which I've pushed the envelope beyond my own better judgement, I believe I'm more cautious and alert after a 1,000-mile day than most motorcyclists out for a casual ride around the neighborhood.

When the rhythm sets in, I don't feel like I'm sitting on top of a motorcycle. Instead, I feel that the machine is an extension of my body, endowing me with superhuman powers. The machine is an extension of my limbs, vesting my feet and hands with unimagined abilities. Yehudi Menuhin once said that playing the violin is like singing through your limbs. I often think about that as I'm riding, and feel that I'm playing Beethoven's Fifth Symphony through the motorcycle.

With the help of earplugs and a good helmet, I fly quietly along just a few feet above the solid surface of the highway. With a flick of my wrist I accelerate quickly around other vehicles. I shift my weight imperceptibly and glide gracefully from one lane to another. I negotiate curves nimbly and confidently, as if the motorcycle were attached to a rail. I'm as agile as a hummingbird, negotiating my way around 18-wheelers, automobiles, and campers, noting the location and relative speed of every vehicle within my field of vision.

I don't forget about potential dangers, and strive to remain alert to other traffic. I don't have a death wish, but once the rhythm sets in I'm frozen to the motorcycle, seduced by the highway, and intoxicated by the awareness that what I'm doing can quickly become fatal if I don't ride competently. With endurance riding comes the responsibility of exercising judgement and care, to avoid harming oneself. With it also comes the obligation to recognize the onset of fatigue, and to deal with it responsibly. Fatigue, like debris on the highway or drunk drivers, is just another of many realities that must be dealt with. Having to stop is usually an unwelcome nuisance. I feel wonderful when I'm back on the motorcycle after a ten-minute stop for gas. I love the sensation of riding so much that continuing on is its own reward.

Endurance riding has often been a subject of criticism from other riders. I'm not surprised that most people don't understand the allure of the sport. A number of riders *claim* to understand it, but don't. Motorcycle journalists are perhaps the worst critics. Except for Bob Higdon, who understands even though he denies it, and Chris Cimino, who has actually *completed* an Iron Butt Rally, they *always* get it wrong. They invariably observe that we have either forgotten (or never knew) what motorcycling is *really* about, citing some worn-out cliche about how much more enjoyable it would be to smell roses.

Bob Higdon, in his foreword to my first book, *Against the Wind*, offered his take on why riders participate in endurance events such as the Iron Butt Rally:

> *The answer could be, in this most sublimely solitary of sports, ironically a question of companionship. The riders rarely see each other, dancing as they do across the country in chaotic, Brownian motion. They're not talking to anyone, except maybe to themselves. If they're not riding, sleeping in the saddle on the side of the road, or eating dinner while standing next to a gas pump at three o'clock in the morning, then they're just wasting time.*
>
> *But think of the end. Think how glorious it will be to get off the bike and not have to count the minutes until you have to strap yourself onto it again. When you turn off the key for the last time, there aren't 100 people on earth who can seriously appreciate what you have undergone. About 40 of them will show up at a motel west of Salt Lake City, looking as pounded as you do. They are the only ones who really know. The rest of us can only guess. You ride this endless ride to be one of them.*

I believe endurance riding is as far removed from traditional motorcycle touring as mountain climbing is from hiking well-worn paths through national parks.

Hiking is enjoyed by many. Only a few climb mountains.

4

Preparation

I purchased my first motorcycle in 1987 at the age of 44. I quickly became interested in riding long distances and gradually increased my endurance to the point where I could comfortably ride more than 1,000 miles in a day. In 1995, I entered my first endurance event, the Iron Butt Rally.

The IBA (Iron Butt Association) conducts the Iron Butt Rally every two years. The rally is the world's premier motorcycle endurance riding event and more than 500 riders vie for the 100 available spots. The rally's catchphrase is "The World's Toughest Motorcycle Competition."

I placed sixth in the 1995 Iron Butt, and was in second place for total miles ridden, logging a little more than 12,000 miles. I enjoyed the Iron Butt so much that I chronicled my participation and experiences in a book, *Against the Wind*.

The rally whetted my appetite for more endurance events. I participated in several 24-hour and 36-hour events, then competed in the 8/48. Participation in nearly a dozen endurance rallies taught me the importance of preparing properly for such a strenuous ride. I expected the 7/49 to be my "ride of a lifetime" and I was committed to prepare properly for it.

The Route

Although I liked the idea of establishing a record for 49-states, the most important aspect of my ride would be to break the existing 48-state record. Therefore, I planned to break the 48-

state record before attempting to add the 49th. This meant I'd have to end my ride somewhere in the Pacific Northwest.

After some research, I decided to start from Kittery, Maine, and end the ride in Kennewick, Washington. Kennewick is a relatively easy-to-reach city near the southern border between Washington and Oregon. More importantly, it's very close to the home of Dale "Warchild" Wilson, a close friend and Iron Butt veteran who could help me plan the conclusion of the 48-state ride and launch me on the final leg to Alaska.

I selected Hyder, Alaska, the southernmost city in Alaska accessible by road, as the termination point of the 49-state ride. As an extra bonus, Hyder is about 1,000 miles west of Edmonton, Alberta, Canada, giving me about a week before the start of the Alberta 2000 Endurance Rally, which I wanted to attend for the third consecutive year.

I divided the trip into six "legs." The first four legs were punctuated by four-hour rest periods at pre-arranged motels in South Carolina, Oklahoma, Nebraska, and Utah, respectively. The fifth leg terminated with Washington as the 48th state, and the sixth terminated in Alaska. Although I expected to be very tired during the last two legs, I didn't want to be locked into a scheduled rest that might interfere with breaking the record. I decided to rest only when absolutely necessary on the final two legs.

I used several different software packages as tools to help plan my route. Two of these packages included an "optimize" feature that identified the shortest route possible for a list of cities to be visited. I also selected potential intermediate stops, a process which involved a lot of trial and error. Many cities were chosen at random, but some were selected deliberately. I knew that Century, Florida, would be a good choice, as it would permit me to visit Florida without having to travel very far into the state. Needles was a great candidate for California, and Texarkana would enable me to hit Texas and Arkansas while stopping at only one city.

The first time I ran the optimization feature on my initial selection of stops, the program produced a 48-state route that was 1,000 miles longer than the record Crane/Kneebone ride. I studied my route for opportunities to reduce the distance, then ran the optimization program again. This aspect of the planning continued for several months until I developed a route that I couldn't improve upon any further. Then I focused on identifying nearby business establishments I could count on for the required proof of purchase. Several of the trip planning packages provided this information, too.

I've adopted the practice of developing "route slips" for use in following an intended course on endurance rallies. I place the strips, upon which simple directions have been written, into my tank bag where maps are usually placed. I believe its easier for me to read the directions, which are printed in a large font, rather than try to refer to maps while I'm riding. I prepared six pages of route slips.

I also prepared several hundred copies of a "poop sheet" that I could distribute to anyone who exhibited interest in my ride. This would save me countless boring repetitions of what I was attempting, freeing my mind for more important matters at rest stops. On one side of the sheet I had printed a map of North America, with the intended route highlighted. Beneath the map were a few paragraphs that explained my 7/49 ride. On the opposite side I listed checkpoints and expected arrival times.

The Schedule

I wanted to get the traffic-congested northeast behind me while I was as fresh and alert as possible. I also wanted to select a starting date that would minimize the possibility of encountering bad weather and which would not put me on the highways during a holiday weekend.

Fran Crane and Mike Kneebone started their 48-state, record ride from Pendleton, Oregon, at 8:00 a.m., presumably after a good night's sleep. Because I planned to begin in the northeast and wished to avoid traffic in that part of the country, I decided to depart at 7:00 p.m. on a Sunday evening, June 7, 1998. My only Saturday night riding, when I'm most concerned about drunk drivers, would occur in the most remote areas of British Columbia, on my final push to Hyder, Alaska. This starting time would also mean that my final hours of riding would be done during daylight.

When my wife Barbara first realized that I was actually going to attempt this ride, she asked me how confident I was of success based on my experience in other endurance events. Her concern was that I would have to average 150 miles more per day than I had averaged in the 1995 Iron Butt Rally.

I pointed out that the Iron Butt was an eleven-day event and that I didn't begin to really tire until the last two or three days.

"Barb, this is only going to be a seven-day ride," I reasoned. "I'll be done with it by the time I'd normally begin to wind down on an Iron Butt."

My argument was so convincing that Barbara used it to reassure my mother at the beginning of my ride.

The Witnesses

Iron Butt Association (IBA) rules for breaking the 48-state record required that I secure the signatures of at least two objective witnesses in each state. The witnesses were required to sign a form that included my photograph, as well as validating my odometer reading, license plate, and the time and date of my arrival at the location. At the beginning and end of the ride, the IBA also required that I obtain the signatures of two police officers. If police officers couldn't be located, four IBA member signatures could be used, but an explanatory letter would have to be submitted, explaining why police signatures were not used. I decided to take no chances at the Kittery checkpoint, and to have both police and IBA member signatures. Since there was no police station in Hyder, I planned to use IBA witnesses there.

It was important to insure that witnesses were reliable enough to respond to a verification request. If they failed to provide the verification, it would be as if I had no witness at all. Because the reliability of witnesses was so important, I enlisted friends and riders from the long distance riding community. In addition, this strategy would save me valuable time; I wouldn't have to find strangers on location and persuade them to help me. I also knew that I would have more incentive to stay on schedule if I knew friends were waiting for me.

I developed a web site to generate interest in my ride and to provide a way for volunteers to sign up electronically. The site was also useful for generating interest in *Against the Wind,* my book about the 1995 Iron Butt Rally.

I've often found that if I wish to do something that is very difficult and requires significant effort, it's helpful to announce my intentions to friends. Once having gone on record, I'm reluctant to risk the embarrassment of not following through. When I wrote the 8/48 article for Steve Chalmers, I announced my intention to accomplish a 7/49. After asking friends and fellow endurance riding enthusiasts to arrange their schedules to be present at checkpoints, it would have been even more difficult to retreat from the plan.

At first I was concerned about not attracting enough volunteers. However, I soon realized that, at least for some states, I had too many. I thought it would be wise to obtain commitments from three or four witnesses, in case someone had to cancel at the last moment, but I didn't want to have to take the time at the checkpoints to have more than a few people sign the documentation. I established an "official witness list" and a "backup list" and encouraged those interested to come to the checkpoint, but explained that I couldn't use more than three or four "official" witnesses at each location.

Soon after, I began receiving suggestions to help with the planning. Many volunteers offered to scout the checkpoint locations to recommend a suitable meeting place. For example, my route dictated that I be in the remote, mountainous area of southwestern Virginia after about my first thirty hours on the road. I wasn't familiar with that area, so I wrote a good friend, four-time Iron Butt Rally veteran Harold Brooks. I told him of my idea to use Ewing, Virginia, as a checkpoint and asked him to check it out. Even though Ewing is more than 270 miles from Harold's home near Lynchburg, I knew he would welcome an excuse to ride through the Blue Ridge Mountains:

Ron,

Got a chance to ride to Ewing today, here's the deal:

When you come into Virginia on US 58 from Tennessee (yes, you'll hit a little corner of Tennessee there) the road is two lanes for about two miles. After that it becomes a four lane, silky smooth, divided highway! About five miles into Virginia, there's an Exxon on the left; a little Mom and Pop operation. They told me they stayed open until 11:00 p.m. during the week, but after the weather warms, it may go 'til midnight.

About ten miles past this at Ewing, there's another Exxon on the right, they stay open 'til midnight. Maybe I could bribe one of them to stay open a little longer if you are running late. If not, the next possibility would be Gate City, sixty miles to the east. Let me know what you think.

Harold

Another friend, Art Holland, rode to Luna Pier, Michigan, where I had planned to check off the Great Lakes State, and warned me about construction on I-75 that would probably delay me. Instead, he suggested Ottawa Lake, a location that was easier to reach and which resulted in fewer miles. Christian Dehner recommended my Kentucky stop and provided detailed instructions for getting to it. Pete Dean planned my stop in Minnesota.

And so it went during the months that preceded my ride, with numerous suggestions and recommendations to help make my ride successful.

Some volunteers asked if I they could ride part of the way with me. Scott Ward of Hastings, Minnesota, volunteered to be a witness in Fargo, North Dakota, and asked if he could ride there with me from Minnesota. Scott wanted to use the opportunity to earn an IBA SaddleSore Certificate, a document issued by the Iron Butt Association for riding at least 1,000 miles in 24 hours. He wanted me to be *his* witness. As my North Dakota stop was planned for about 3:00 a.m., I was pleased to have a volunteer.

At first, I didn't have volunteers for some of the more remote areas such as Montana, Wyoming, or the Dakotas. I made a list of some special friends and hard-core riders to whom I would appeal for these "hardship" locations. Before I had to ask, however, Bill Weyher, winner of the Utah 1088 Rally in 1996, approached me with an offer:

"DeVern Gerber and I have talked about your ride and we'll volunteer to ride with you to be witnesses in Montana, South Dakota, and Wyoming. Just let us know when and where you want to meet and we'll take care of those states." I gladly accepted their offer but promised to continue to try to recruit additional witnesses so they wouldn't have to carry so much of the load.

The most remote location where witnesses would be required was Hyder, Alaska, nearly 1,000 miles from the "lower 48." As it turned out, it was easier to arrange for witnesses in Hyder than in many locations in the contiguous states. I had made a lot of friends in Edmonton, Alberta, Canada, over the years as a result of my participation in the Alberta 2000 Endurance Rallies. Tracy DesLaurier, the rallymaster of the Alberta 2000, and Vince Kretzul, the president of Black Gold Beemers in Edmonton, volunteered to be in Hyder. Herb Anderson, who competed with me in the 8/48, the 1997 Iron Butt Rally, and several Alberta 2000s, also volunteered. Alberta 2000 veteran Chris Baldwin of Vancouver, British Columbia, signed up too.

Wally Jordan, a friend from Prescott, Arizona, asked me to hold his name in reserve until I had identified a location where I was having difficulty finding a volunteer. "Ron, I'll be anywhere you want me to be," Wally offered in an e-mail message. Seventy-six years young and the winner of the 1996 Alberta 2000 Endurance Rally, Wally agreed to be in South Carolina.

The Internet
One of the most important tools that my wife Barbara and I would use during my ride was my web site and the Internet's LDRIDER list. The Long Distance Rider List provides a means for Internet subscribers, primarily long-distance riding enthusiasts, to broadcast messages to other subscribers on the list. If

an e-mail message is sent to the appropriate LDRIDER address, all members of the list receive a copy of the message. Any
rider can comment on or respond to the message, and have his
or her response automatically broadcast to all subscribers.

I knew that many of my friends who volunteered to be witnesses were subscribers to LDRIDER and that the list would be
an invaluable tool for keeping them and the entire endurance
riding community current on the progress of my ride.

However, there were also volunteers and other interested
observers who were not subscribers to LDRIDER. Therefore,
my web site served as the primary vehicle for communicating
the progress of my ride. I set up pages that corresponded to the
legs of my ride and taught Barbara how to make basic updates
to the pages. Each page contained a copy of my route map for
the leg and would be augmented with textual updates as the
ride progressed.

Several weeks before my planned departure, I sent an e-
mail message to the volunteers to review how I hoped the
checkpoint operations would be conducted. The message included a description of the tasks I would have to perform at
each stop. I announced the plan for Barbara to periodically update the web site to keep witnesses informed of progress or delays, until she had to leave for Hyder to meet me. I suggested
that as long as it was between 8:00 a.m. and 10:00 p.m., someone from the checkpoints should call Barbara with an update on
my progress, and I provided a toll-free number for this purpose.

The Guinness Book of World Records
All of my planning had been done on the basis of rules published on the Iron Butt web site. To insure that Guinness would
recognize my record, and that there hadn't been a change in the
rules since their publication on the Iron Butt web site, I wrote
to Guinness. Several weeks later, I received a letter stating
they would not recognize my record:

> *Shortly after publication of the 1995 edition, the*
> *editors of the Guinness Book of World Records decided*
> *to retire a number of place-to-place driving records for*
> *both cars and motorcycles. We felt that there was an*

unacceptable risk of fatigue-related accidents
occurring during these record attempts, and we were
concerned that future participants might be tempted to
commit traffic or speed violations in order to break the
existing records. Therefore, we will be unable to
recognize or publish records in these categories in the
future.

This didn't discourage me from continuing with my plans. After all, the IBA would validate my record and the endurance riding community would recognize it. If I succeeded, I could claim to have broken the previous Guinness record, even if they would no longer acknowledge it.

The Bike
When I first planned the 7/49, I intended to use my '95 BMW K1100LT. The motorcycle had been extremely reliable but had over 80,000 miles on the odometer after I competed in the 1997 Iron Butt. In spite of my affection for the bike, I knew that a bike with so many miles would be more likely to experience a component failure than a new one. With all of the time and planning that I was putting into the 7/49, I wanted to do as much as I could to mitigate the risk of mechanical failure.

I purchased a new 1996 K1100LT. Except for the model year, the bike was an exact duplicate of my '95. Even the graphite color was the same. I purchased the bike and ordered a vanity license plate, *KLONE,* which stood for "K Bike Clone."

I had wanted to put at least 10,000 miles on the new motorcycle before the record attempt, but my work schedule didn't permit the break-in riding I'd hoped for prior to the 7/49.

Due to my previous catastrophes with lost receipts, one of the most important aspects of the planning had to do with the precautions I would take to insure that I wouldn't lose receipts or other documentation. I was also worried that material might get misplaced or lost while being handled by witnesses.

I printed witness forms on heavy paper stock and placed them in a 3-ring binder that could be closed with a zipper. I secured the 3-ring binder to the inside of the rear luggage compartment of my motorcycle with a steel cable. The cable was long enough to permit the volunteers to rest the binder on the rear of the motorcycle while they signed the forms, but it could not be taken from the motorcycle.

I obtained a zippered currency bag for storing receipts and covered one side of it with Velcro. I then placed Velcro inside the lid of my rear luggage compartment so the zippered receipt bag could be secured there. I didn't intend to remove the bag until the ride was over.

The Body
In April, well before the planned start of the ride, I made a commitment to get into better physical condition, which included losing weight. When I departed for Kittery ten weeks later, I had shed more than 20 pounds and was running at least 20 miles per week.

Although I like coffee, I stopped drinking it, as well as soft drinks containing caffeine. I didn't want to depend on drugs of any kind to accomplish the ride. Whenever I was tempted to fall off the wagon, I tried to imagine the frustration, disappointment, and sense of failure that I would feel if I failed to accomplish what I had announced I would do.

The Suit
The choice of riding suits presented a dilemma. I owned a one-piece Aerostich Roadcrafter, a suit that is favored by many hard-core, long-distance touring enthusiasts. I loved it and considered it my single most important item of motorcycling equipment—until I found that it leaked in prolonged, heavy rain. During the first two months of 1998, I took two long trips of over 1,000 miles each, in which a lot of the riding was done in very heavy rain; in both cases, the suit leaked badly. With these experiences in mind, I didn't trust the suit to keep me dry.

Paul Golde at Intersport Fashions West, the distributor for First Gear apparel, offered to provide a Solo Expedition one-piece suit that he promised would keep me dry. "I'd be very interested in an evaluation of the suit by someone who rides the way you do," Paul remarked. "I'll send you a suit, but I'd like you to report back and let me know what you like or don't like about it."

The Final Glitch

To minimize the amount of time I would have to take off from work, I used weekends to move my motorcycle closer to Kittery. A month before the ride, I rode *KLONE* to Baltimore, parked it in my mother's garage, and flew back to Texas. Two weeks later, when I was scheduled to speak at a rally in Thurmont, Maryland, I flew back to Maryland, gave my speech, and moved the motorcycle to a BMW dealer for service. I returned to Texas, and planned to return to Maryland a week later to pick it up and ride to Kittery.

The day before I was to return to Maryland for the motorcycle, however, I called the shop to check on the status of the service work.

"When we removed your rear wheel, four of the five bolts securing the wheel to the motorcycle were loose and about to fall out," the mechanic reported. "The remaining bolt was only finger tight. Because the bolts were so loose, the vibration caused the threads on the bolts to become stripped. You're lucky the threads on the wheel weren't stripped. That would have cost you a lot of money, not to mention the risk of having the wheel come off."

I immediately thought about the wheel work that I had performed on the bike just before I rode it to Maryland. I wanted to have the wheels "powder chromed" to dress it up and to make them easier to clean. The shop that performed the work was the last shop to work on the bike before I left for Baltimore.

"That's not the worst of your problems," the mechanic continued. "When we removed the front wheel, the bearings were so loose they fell out. After mounting your new tire, we had to use LockTite when we replaced the bearings."

I explained the service work that had been performed on the wheels.

"The proper procedure for removing the bearing from the wheel is to heat the wheel first. If the shop didn't know what they were doing, they may have forced the bearing out before they powder-coated the wheel. That would have caused the fit to be too loose when the bearings were replaced," he continued.

"How big a problem have I got," I asked. "I'm planning to ride the bike through 49 states after I pick it up tomorrow. Is the LockTite going to be adequate?"

"We can't advise you that it's a safe solution for something like that," the mechanic continued. "I'm sure you understand, what with legal liability issues and all."

"Look pal, I understand the legal implications. I'm not going to ask you if the motorcycle is safe. Let's put it this way: If the motorcycle were yours, would you ride it for 10,000 miles?"

There was a long hesitation before his reply. I already knew what I wanted his answer to be.

"No, I'd replace the front wheel. That's what I think you should do."

"Do you have one in stock?" I asked.

"Let me check."

I was on hold for at least five minutes before he returned. I thought about the potential this problem had to ruin the plans that had been under development for a year and a half. If I delayed the trip, I would have to put it off for at least a week, as an important element of my strategy was to leave Maine on a Sunday evening to avoid New York and New England traffic. I also didn't want to ride in populated areas during a weekend. And I would no longer be able to count on the availability of all the volunteers.

"No, we don't have another wheel here," the mechanic said as he returned to the phone. "I also checked to see if we had a used one, but no luck. I suggest that you order one from some BMW dealer along the way. It should only take a few days for them to get one."

If I did opt to order a wheel, the logical place to have it replaced would be Hattiesburg, Mississippi—the only BMW dealership that I had planned to use as a checkpoint. I tried again to get an accurate assessment of the risk I would be taking if I undertook the trip without replacing the wheel.

"Well look, to be real honest with you, LockTite holds real good. We even use it sometimes on parts of gears inside the engine and the stuff works well. If you want to take off with it, you can check the wheel every now and then and you'll know if it's

getting loose. Just put the bike on the center stand, have someone place their weight on the rear wheel, and grab the front tire
with two hands and give it a good shake. You'll be able to tell if
it's starting to loosen up."

"Thanks. Will the motorcycle be ready to roll the first thing
in the morning?" I asked. "I'm planning on flying in tonight and
I'll want to get the bike as soon as you open."

"No problem. The bike's ready now."

I hung up the phone, sat back in my chair, and considered
this very unwelcome, last-minute development.

"Damn!" I thought. "By having vanity work performed on
my wheels, I had broken the Iron Butt Association's rule #5 for
safe, long-distance touring: Avoid adding accessories or doing
maintenance immediately before a trip.

"I don't want to have to postpone this ride," I thought. "But I
don't want to fail by knowingly attempting it on a defective motorcycle."

Damn! Even if I proceeded and didn't have a problem with
the wheel, I had learned during two Iron Butt Rallies that any
minor aggravation is magnified during such a rigorous event.
Subjecting myself to additional concern or worry would mean
additional stress, and that would mean tiring a little sooner. I
had formulated my own new rule to add to the Iron Butt
Association's list of "28 Long Distance Tips." Rule # 29: Eliminate *all* distractions and potential irritants *before* the ride, no
matter how minor they seem.

One thing was certain. If I proceeded, I couldn't let Barbara
know about this. Although she worries when I participate in an
activity like this, she's always been understanding and supportive. One of the things she's always appreciated is that I use
common sense and good equipment. I didn't want her to worry
about a potential problem with the wheel.

I decided to proceed as planned. I would check the wheel
frequently. If it became unsafe, I would ask one of the volunteers with an LT to swap wheels.

It might sound presumptuous for me to count on this type of
help, but I knew that if the success of my ride depended on it, I
had several friends with LTs who would *insist* on the swap.

Randell Hendricks would be waiting for me in Texarkana. Mike
Cornett was planning to be in Illinois and Adam Wolkoff would
be in North Dakota. Ira Agins would be in Santa Fe on his
brand new LT. If I made it to Wendover, Utah, or anywhere
within a few hundred miles of Salt Lake City, I could count on
Steve Chalmers or Gary Eagan to bring me a wheel. George
Barnes, Bill Weyher, and DeVern Gerber would be waiting in
Montana, all mounted on LTs. And there were others. It's nice
to have such friends.

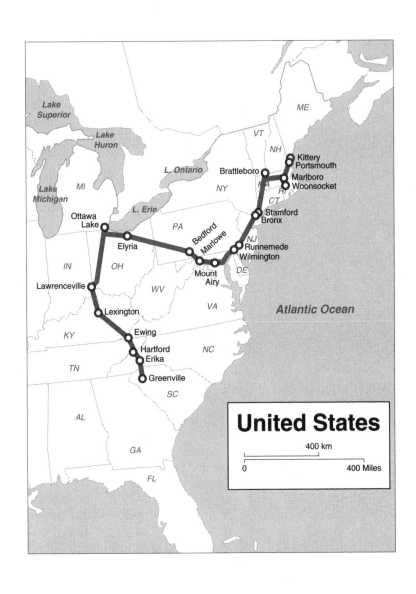

United States

400 km

0   400 Miles

5

Maine to South Carolina

---

1 - Maine

I arrived in Kittery on Saturday evening, June 6. I slept well on Saturday night and took a short nap on Sunday afternoon. I had a very vivid dream that reflected the importance the coming ride held for me. I sent Barbara an e-mail message:

> *I just awoke from a good 90-minute nap. I guess you know that you actually slept if you had a dream (or, a nightmare). You and I were flying back from Maine to Dallas, and when we landed I realized I had left my laptop computer in Maine in the motel room. I started trying to figure out how to get it shipped back to me, then realized the reason I left it there with my riding gear was that I wasn't supposed to fly back to Dallas with you. I was supposed to stay to begin the 7/49.*

> *I began cursing and headed for the ticket counter to buy a ticket back to Maine, and was disgusted because I'd have to pay an exorbitant price for a ticket purchased at the last minute. When I looked at my watch, I realized I was to begin the 7/49 in an hour. This screwed up everything, because witnesses would show up and I wouldn't be there. Then I woke up.*

> *I hope this doesn't portend anything.*

Later, I called Barbara for what I knew would likely be the last leisurely conversation we'd have for a week. She had read my message about the dream and encouraged me not to worry about it.

"It's natural that you would have an anxiety dream like that this soon before your departure. After all, look how long you've looked forward to this," she reassured me.

I used the hours that remained to visit the Kittery area. I rode a few miles south on Route 1 to Portsmouth, New Hampshire, and located the gasoline station where volunteer Ed Farrell suggested we meet. I visited a small souvenir shop and purchased small state flags for Maine and Alaska and fastened them to the bike's antenna.

I rode by the Kittery police station several times. Each time, the sight of patrol cars in the parking lot comforted me. "I shouldn't have any difficulty finding officers to sign the forms," I thought. I also noticed that the police station was adjacent to a Getty gasoline station and convenience store.

"Great. I'll get the witness and police officers to sign the forms, stop at the Getty station for fuel, and be on my way."

Technically, the only witness signatures I would need to launch the trip would be the officers in Kittery. But I wanted to play it safe and have the signatures of some IBA members at each checkpoint.

I've participated in a lot of motorcycle endurance rallies over the years. They all have been characterized by a similar pattern of activity in the hours preceding the event. Riders visit with each other to pass the time. They inspect each other's motorcycles, debate the pros and cons of the latest navigation equipment, radar detectors, tires, or radio equipment. The beginning of this event was lonely by comparison.

At about 4:30 I did some last minute grocery shopping and packing. I purchased a half-dozen bananas, a few bags of trail mix, and a gallon of spring water.

When I returned to the motel, I emptied all of my luggage and the contents of my tank bag on the bed and repacked everything. I've developed a system of packing that doesn't vary from one endurance event to another. Items I expect to use frequently, like earplugs, note pads, spare gloves, and a tire pressure gauge are stored in the top of my tank bag. Items I may want to locate quickly, but which I won't need while on the move, like face shields, extra ear plugs, lip balm, flashlight, tank bag, rain cover, and Swiss Army knife are stored in the lower, zippered section of the tank bag.

The motorcycle leans to the left when parked on the sidestand, making it difficult to remove items from the left side case without having them fall out when the cover is opened. The first aid kit, tire repair kit, flares, duct tape, and other infrequently used items are stowed there. Extra gloves, the electric vest, and electric chaps are packed on the right. I use the rear luggage compartment for storing the logbook, maps, camera, and tripod.

I checked out of the room and rode down Route 1, past the police station, and stopped at Joe's Clam Shack for the last real meal I expected to have for the next week. Although I hadn't planned to leave until about 7:00 p.m., I became impatient and headed for the police station after dinner. Jeff Small, Ed Farrell, Howard Chain, and John McKay were already waiting.

But there were no patrol cars.

Maine starting checkpoint: Howard Chain, Jeff Watts, Ron, Ed Farrell, John McKay (in front), Jeff Small, and Anne Small.

After greeting the witnesses, I walked across the parking lot to the station house. A dispatcher was sitting in a small room behind bulletproof glass. A microphone and a panel of radio equipment were spread before her.

"Can I help you?" she asked.

"I hope so," I replied. "I was hoping to get the signatures of some police officers for some witness forms."

"Oh, you're the guy who's planning to do some record ride around the country or something," she replied with a pleasant smile. "Someone stopped in here earlier and was telling me about it. It won't be long, I'll radio an officer and ask him to stop by."

"I hope it isn't too much trouble, but actually I need the signatures of two officers."

"Well, I'll just have to radio for two of them then, won't I?" she smiled. "That won't be a problem."

I walked back to the motorcycle, encouraged by this early sign of cooperation. I removed my logbook from the tour pack and began the initial round of witness signings. I gave each of the witnesses a copy of the "poop sheet" to review while we waited for the police officers.

I wasn't concerned about having the clock running at this point, as I understood that the clock would start based on the time stamped on the gasoline receipt I would obtain before heading for New Hampshire.

Soon, Officers Peter Gscheidle and Gary Berggren arrived. I explained what I was about to do and handed them copies of my flyer. They were interested in the ride and were pleased to complete the witness forms.

With witness forms complete, I removed my camera and tripod from the rear luggage compartment and prepared to take my first group shot, using the camera's self-timing feature. I planned to repeat this exercise at each stop so I could publish a series of 49 photographs on my web site. I was prepared to eliminate this aspect of the routine if I found it required too much time or became troublesome, but I wanted to give it a try.

Howard Chain examined my motorcycle closely, then noticed the Maine and Alaska State flags attached to my antenna.

"Those will look pretty ragged and threadbare by the end of the week," Howard remarked.

"Yeah, and so will Ron," Ed Farrell quipped.

Soon after I announced plans for the 7/49, Howard signed on to help and he had offered to escort me for the first few states. A real estate developer and investor in New Hampshire and Florida, Howard is in the enviable position of being able to ride in New England in the summer and Florida in the winter. He first became interested in long-distance riding after visiting the Gorham, Maine, checkpoint of the 1995 Iron Butt Rally. He's on the waiting list for the 1999 Iron Butt.

I returned the camera and tripod to the luggage compartment and rode the few hundred feet to the Getty station to purchase gasoline. I would be stopping again in New Hampshire after riding less than five miles, so I purchased only a few gallons and walked into the store to pay the $2.50 I owed. Howard followed me.

When I handed the clerk my credit card, he glanced at his remote readout, then looked at me, then back at the readout. He looked at me again with a look of chagrin.

I realized that he probably wasn't permitted to accept a credit card for payment of such a small purchase.

"It costs us an extra fifty cents to run a credit card purchase for less than $5.00," he apologized.

"Look, I normally wouldn't try to put such a small purchase on a credit card, but it's important that I have a time- and date-stamped, computer-generated receipt for this purchase. I'll be happy to pay the fifty-cent charge," I offered.

"Well, there's a better way we can do this," the clerk responded, trying to be helpful. "I'll just ring up a charge for $6.00 and give you $3.50 in cash back. How's that?"

"So long as I get a computer-generated receipt for the purchase, that works for me," I replied.

I examined the receipt to insure that the date and time were clearly legible and thanked the clerk for his help. The timestamp read "6:26 p.m.," the start of my 49-state ride.

As I neared the motorcycle, I could imagine it beckoning to me. *Come on, let's go, let's go!* KLONE seemed to be saying.

I mounted up and headed for New Hampshire. I felt, for the first time, that the trip was finally under way.

Day	State	Miles Ridden	Miles to Go
1	1	0	8,798

2 - New Hampshire

It required less than five minutes to arrive at the New Hampshire checkpoint and less than ten minutes more to repeat the signing, fueling, and photography session.

As I was preparing to leave, Howard approached with his hand extended. "Here, Ron, take these toll tokens for the New Hampshire Turnpike. I'll lead the way, but we'll get through the toll gates faster if you just toss one of these in the hopper when we pass through."

"Thanks, Howard, but I'm afraid I've got to do this the old-fashioned way," I explained. "Each time I pay a toll, whether at a toll road or a bridge, I'm required to obtain a receipt and make an entry in the log book. I'm planning to use the right-hand lane of the tollbooths so I can pull over easily to make the log entry and store the receipt.

New Hampshire checkpoint: Howard Chain, Anne Small, Todd Crowley, Jeff Small, Ron, and Ed Farrell.

"Gotcha," Howard responded as he gave me a 'thumbs up' sign. "How fast do you want to travel the Turnpike?"

"Just a tad faster than the flow of traffic."

"You've got it," Howard responded.

Soon after we got on the New Hampshire Turnpike, a slight drizzle began to fall. "Thank heavens I don't have to worry about becoming wet on this trip," I thought, as I zipped the front of the Solo Expedition suit and settled comfortably into the relatively short 75-mile route to the Massachusetts checkpoint.

Day	State	Miles Ridden	Miles to Go
1	2	3	8,795

3 - Massachusetts

When we pulled into the Exxon Tiger Mart, Jeffrey and Jamison Luke and Camela Pryor were waiting.

Massachusetts checkpoint: Ron, Jeffrey Luke, Camela Pryor, and Jamison Luke.

Rhode Island checkpoint: Michael Thrasher, Brian Roth, Tom Maloney, and Ron.

As I was refueling, I noticed I had already lost the Maine flag that had been attached to my antenna, and the Alaska flag was badly tattered.

"You've already logged three states in a little over an hour. At this rate, you'll have the 48-states done by noon tomorrow," Howard quipped.

I asked Howard to take the obligatory picture of me with the Massachusetts witnesses, thanked them, and headed for Rhode Island. Howard called Barbara to provide her with the first of many updates she would receive and post to my web site during the next week.

Day	State	Miles Ridden	Miles to Go
1	3	71	8,724

4 - Rhode Island

Tom Maloney was familiar with the route I would take from Massachusetts to Rhode Island, and then to Vermont. Before I left Texas, he'd provided me with detailed instructions for reaching the Mobil station in Woonsocket. When I arrived,

Brian Roth and Michael Thrasher were waiting. Tom Maloney didn't arrive until I had already taken a photo and was preparing to depart.

"Oh great, I'm only 45 minutes early and I almost miss the party," Tom said as he dismounted.

"Hey, no problem," I replied. "I got an early start because I was eager to get going. Let me set up the camera again and get a shot with you in it, too."

I repeated the photographic routine, then asked Tom to sign a witness form.

Day	State	Miles Ridden	Miles to Go
1	4	103	8,695

By the time I reached I-290 near Worcester, it was raining steadily. I removed my radar detector from its mounting bracket, unzipped the tank bag, and stuffed it inside.

I was traveling only a little faster than the speed limit, but wasn't concerned about attracting the attention of the highway patrol. I believe it's less likely you'll be stopped while it is raining, simply because most law enforcement officers would prefer not to write citations while standing in the rain.

A few minutes after getting onto I-91 for the final 20 miles to Brattleboro, however, my brisk riding style caught the attention of a very conscientious Massachusetts State Trooper. He decided to stop me for a discussion, rain or no rain.

I pulled the motorcycle to the side of the road and placed it on the sidestand. I removed my gloves, helmet, and earplugs by the time the trooper approached me, flashlight under one arm.

"May I see your driver's license please," the trooper asked in a dull but polite monotone.

As I extracted my wallet from my breast pocket and removed my driver's license and registration, the officer exhibited mild interest in the motorcycle as he ran the beam of his flashlight over it. He studied the instrument panel. I assumed he was interested in whether the bike was equipped with a radar detector.

When I planned the ride, I didn't intend to ride fast enough to be stopped for speeding. If stopped, I didn't intend to acknowledge that I was trying to set any records.

"What are you doing out here on a motorcycle in this rain?" the officer asked.

"I'm on vacation and I'm just trying to get in some riding. I don't have a lot of opportunities to ride, so when I get the time off, I like to stay on the motorcycle. It looks as though I let the speed get a little higher than I should have."

There was no response to my confession.

"Did you ride all the way here from Texas?" the officer asked as he examined my license.

"Yes."

"Where are you heading?"

"Brattleboro."

"What's in Brattleboro?"

"A motel," I answered.

I was sure there was a motel somewhere in Brattleboro, even if I had no intention of using it.

"I've been on the road a long time and was a little eager to get to Brattleboro before it gets too late," I continued.

The officer continued to examine my license, turning it over several times and looking at the front and back of it. I hoped he would give me a warning, and was trying to decide if I would enhance my chances by asking for a break, or if I would be better off remaining silent. The officer had not mentioned how fast I was going or why he stopped me.

The officer continued to examine my license for a few more seconds.

"OK, go on. But drive a little slower," the officer said, as he returned my license and registration.

"Thanks a lot. I appreciate this, officer," I answered.

The trooper nodded without smiling, returned to his patrol car and waited until I pulled from the shoulder of the road. Then he pulled out, passed me, and continued north toward Brattleboro.

I wondered what it was about the encounter that "worked" this time. Perhaps he felt sorry for a guy older than his father who was trying to enjoy his vacation while riding a motorcycle late at night in the cold rain. I'd like to think he was exercising judgement, rather than acting like an automaton—that he discriminated between someone who was endangering those he was responsible for protecting and someone who was simply in a hurry. It probably helped that I didn't waste his time or insult his intelligence by questioning why I was pulled over.

After visiting Brattleboro, I would return on this same route to Connecticut. This was the only part of the trip where I would backtrack after visiting a checkpoint. I knew I would have to take it easy from here to Brattleboro and back along this route. I couldn't expect any mercy if I were to have the misfortune of being stopped again by the same trooper.

I traveled more slowly for the next hour or so.

5 - Vermont

Earlier in the day, Harry Pendexter rode to Brattleboro to be sure he could find the checkpoint. It was then he discovered that the station would close before my scheduled arrival. The

Vermont checkpoint: Ron, Kathleen Boyer, Tom Mangieri, and Harry Pendexter.

attendant gave Harry directions to another station nearby that would be open when I arrived.

Harry called Barbara, who sent me an e-mail message about a half hour before the start of my ride, but I had already shut down my computer for the week.

Harry met Tom Mangieri and Kathleen Boyer at the checkpoint and suggested that they go to the alternate station. Not sure that I received the message from Barbara, Harry waited at the bottom of the ramp where I was planning to exit the highway.

Harry later wrote in an e-mail to LDRIDER:

I positioned myself to see down the interstate so I would have about a minute to get to the end of the off ramp from the time I saw him.

Right on time, 10:30 p.m., single headlight—long dash to the exit, here he comes, I'm excited! I wave my flashlight at him, he's slowing down. What the hell is this! It's a Ford Escort with one headlight and no marker lights. Padiddle—got ya! I got a tremendous chuckle out of it!

He came at 11:00 p.m. and I directed him to the other station and went that way myself. Surprising how much can be done in fifteen minutes. Intros all around, Ron filled out his part, went into the store while Tom, his girlfriend, and I filled out witness forms. Ron gassed up, changed from heated vest to fleece shirt, ate a banana, pictures, pictures.

I passed along some info about the Tennessee stop and relayed Ron's response to Barbara by phone after he left.

Fellow Iron Butt Rally veteran Jim Culp had called Barbara to suggest a change in the meeting location for the Tennessee stop, which I was scheduled to make in another 24 hours. Jim had visited the location that I had selected and found that it was relatively isolated and likely to be difficult to find in the dark. He also learned that the station would close at 9:00 p.m. I was scheduled to arrive only a half hour before that,

Connecticut checkpoint: Maurice Donini, Berti Levy, Ron, Bill
Kramer, and Joe Xiques.

so he knew I wouldn't be able to use the location for my Tennessee purchase if I were running late.

I headed for I-91 again, this time to cross the entire state of
Massachusetts and most of Connecticut before reaching the
next checkpoint. The clerks at the station had expressed interest in the happenings, so Harry walked back inside and promised to deliver some photos for display on a bulletin board near
the checkout counter.

Day	State	Miles Ridden	Miles to Go
1	5	239	8,559

6 - Connecticut
I was looking forward to meeting Joe Xiques, who offered to ride
with me through the unfamiliar New York metropolitan area. I
was looking forward to the change of routine his company
would provide. I was also looking forward to meeting the first
man in my life whose last name begins with the letter "X."

As I approached the dark Gulf Station checkpoint in Stamford, I could tell the station was closed. My Connecticut witnesses were waiting nonetheless.

I had expected Joe, Maurice Donini, Ed Haupt and Bill Kramer, but was surprised to also see Berti Levi. Berti had wanted to be a witness, but had been planning a ride from Key West, Florida, to Prudhoe Bay, Alaska, during my 7/49 ride. When other obligations prevented him from making the Prudhoe Bay trip, Berti decided to visit me in Connecticut. The day before, Iron Butt Rally veteran Bill Kramer had finished in second place in the Capitol 1000, a 24-hour endurance event that began and ended in Hagerstown, MD. He was understandably tired and had chosen to drive to the checkpoint in his wife's van rather than on his motorcycle.

After doing the paperwork, the group of us backtracked a few miles on I-95 to purchase gas in Connecticut, and I was on my way again.

On his way home from the checkpoint, Bill struck a deer in Pennsylvania. The impact killed the deer and damaged the van. Since the van was still operative, Bill called his wife and arranged to meet her for breakfast so that he could explain the damage to her vehicle.

Day	State	Miles Ridden	Miles to Go
1	6	401	8,397

7 - New York

I don't enjoy riding through New York City on a motorcycle. But whenever I enter the city, especially at night, I'm fascinated by the hundreds of towering apartment buildings with thousands of lighted windows. I usually try to envisage what might be occurring in the dwellings as I pass. What type of people live there? What are they doing at this moment?

I was reminded of the words of Charles Dickens in *A Tale of Two Cities:* "A wonderful fact to reflect upon, that every human creature is constituted to be that profound secret and mystery to every other. A solemn consideration, when I enter a great city by night, that every one of those darkly clustered houses encloses its own secret; that every room in every one of them encloses its own secret; that every beating heart in the hundreds of thousands of breasts there, is, in some of its imaginings, a secret to the heart nearest it!"

Since I spend more time on the motorcycle in rural settings than I do in urban ones, I more often speculate about what is happening in the homes that I pass in small communities. But I'm always reminded of Dickens' words when I enter New York.

Gary Johnson, Keith and Mark Sproul, and Jeffrey Hicken were waiting for me at the Mobil station in the Bronx. Jeffrey, an advertising art director, had just completed a 6,000-mile ride of his own. Two weeks earlier, he had taken delivery of his new Harley-Davidson motorcycle in California and my checkpoint was to be his last stop.

Gary Johnson, another Iron Butt Rally veteran, had just participated in the Capitol 1000.

While I was refueling, Mark introduced me to his identical twin brother, Keith. Mark and Keith married identical twin sis-

New York checkpoint: Jeffrey Hicken, Gary Johnson, Ron, Keith Sproul, and Mark Sproul.

ters, Carol and Debbie, respectively, in a double-ring ceremony. Mark and Keith, as well as their father, ride Gold Wings. Carol and Debbie ride behind their husbands, although Carol occasionally rides in Mark's sidecar. Tonight, Keith was riding in the sidecar.

I had recruited father and son teams, brothers, and husbands and wives. But Mark and Keith Sproul were the only set of identical twins on my list.

Not only do all the Sprouls ride, they are ham radio operators, too. Mark has offered to set me up for the 1999 Iron Butt Rally with radio tracking equipment so enthusiasts can monitor my route on the Internet as the rally progresses.

As the group departed for New Jersey, Jeffrey Hicken and the Sproul brothers joined us for the trip across the Cross-Bronx Expressway.

Day	State	Miles Ridden	Miles to Go
1	7	423	8,375

8 - New Jersey

At about 3:15 a.m., Harold Gantz, Tom Coradeschi, and Chris BeHanna rolled into the Texaco station in Runnemede and told the attendants that they were going to wait around for other motorcyclists to arrive. The attendants looked at them like they were nuts, not understanding why so many riders would be there at that time of the morning. The trio had volunteered for the Delaware checkpoint, but had decided to meet me in New Jersey and ride with me to Delaware.

A few minutes later, Walter Barlow and Al Spilotras, my official New Jersey witnesses, joined them. When I arrived with my entourage, Al greeted me with bagels, groceries, and a bottle of cold water.

"Funny, he doesn't *look* crazy," Walter commented to Tom as I was removing my helmet.

The seven of us departed for Delaware.

Day	State	Miles Ridden	Miles to Go
1	8	530	8,268

New Jersey checkpoint: Walter Barlow, Ron, and Alfred Spilotras.

9 - Delaware

I wasn't familiar with the area and wound up leading the group on an unintended side trip. I should have asked one of the Delaware riders to lead the way.

Harold suspected I was off course, but since he was the last guy in formation, he couldn't communicate this to me. When I realized I had missed a turn, I led the group into a service area in Delaware. It didn't matter where we stopped to perform the checkpoint ritual because the witnesses were already with me.

After refueling and getting the logbook signed, we took some pictures and I took off for Maryland alone.

Day	State	Miles Ridden	Miles to Go
1	9	561	8,237

Harold, Tom, and Chris rode back to the "official" Delaware checkpoint to see if any well-wishers may have ventured out to greet me. They found a dark, deserted, closed, Gulf station. If I

Delaware checkpoint: Harold Gantz, Ron, Tom Coradeschi, and Chris BeHanna.

had stopped there as planned, the station would have been of no use to me for getting a sales receipt.

After my ride, Harold shared his thoughts about his participation in my quest.

> *Speaking for myself, I had a great time for the hour or so I rode along in formation with you. It's not every night I can ride along with half a dozen accomplished motorcyclists under a moonlit sky with no other cars on the highway. I'm glad I had a chance to participate (in a small way) during your ride.*

I had been looking forward to riding under the light of the full moon ever since I'd realized that I had unwittingly timed my ride to coincide with it. I remembered a message that Jan Cutler from Reno BMW had sent to LDRIDER several months earlier. Jan had planned a rally, "The Big Bang," for Ely, Nevada, for the weekend of May 30. In Jan's message, he noted that the rally would fall between the full moons of May 11 and June 9. "It's gonna' be dark, boys," Jan warned.

I was happy to be leaving the traffic-congested New England area behind, and expected to be able to see the stars more clearly when I was away from the big cities.

Although I was only about 12 hours into the ride, at least one Internet follower was already expressing doubt that the entire ride could be performed in the allotted time. Jeff Wooddell, recalling the great distances and low-mileage days he had experienced while driving to Alaska five years earlier, sent the following message to LDRIDER:

> *I sincerely hope he makes his entire trip, but I just don't think it's possible to make the Alaska leg in the allotted time. I'll be reading the messages every day and will be pulling for him.*
>
> *Jeff*

10 - Maryland

It was almost 6:00 a.m. when I approached the entrance to the tunnel under the northwest harbor of Baltimore. I grew up not far from this location and knew I was literally within sight of Fort McHenry, the star-shaped fort famous as the birthplace of the American national anthem. It was the valiant defense of Fort McHenry by American forces during a British attack in 1814 that inspired Francis Scott Key to write "The Star-Spangled Banner."

Soon after I exited the I-695 Baltimore Beltway that circles the city and entered I-70 west, the scenery began to improve as I rolled through the beautiful hills and green pastures of western Maryland. It was a bright, sunny morning and I was looking forward to a great day of riding.

When I pulled into the Texaco station and dismounted, Jackie and John Mosmiller were standing in the parking lot with Diane Donaldson and her friend, Dave Choat. Diane commutes to work on her motorcycle every day. She was one of the first to agree to meet me in Maryland and I had been looking forward to meeting her. Louis Caplan and my sister, Carolyn, were there too. Carolyn wanted to be present when I passed through the area, even though she wouldn't qualify as an "objective" witness.

Ron arrives at the Maryland checkpoint (photo by Carolyn Ayres).

Ron gasses up at the Maryland pump (photo by Carolyn Ayres).

Dave Choat and Diane Donaldson fill out the paperwork at the Maryland checkpoint (photo by Carolyn Ayres).

Maryland checkpoint: Dave Choat, Diane Donaldson, Ron, John Mosmiller, Jackie Mosmiller, and Louis Caplan.

Louis, a Motorcycle Safety Foundation (MSF) Instructor, had just finished in seventh place in the Capitol 1000 Endurance Rally. Louis was prepared to sign my forms, even though he had complained to Jackie that his hands were still tired after recently teaching a motorcycle safety course to a class of deaf students. Louis himself is, in fact, hard-of-hearing. He can hear relatively well with hearing aids, but doesn't claim that it's even close to perfect. Although most of his motorcycle students are able to hear, the week before my record ride, Louis taught a class of deaf students. I later asked Louis about his instructing.

"After I took the MSF course and started riding a motorcycle, I felt it was a big change in my life. I really enjoyed riding, and was grateful to the MSF for teaching me. And, deaf people learn better if they learn directly from the person teaching, rather than through an interpreter, or an instructor making animated gestures out on the range. So it's a combination. I feel I have something to offer deaf people who want to learn to ride, plus I like giving something back to the MSF and the motorcycling community."

Barbara summarized the first twelve hours for my web site followers:

Monday, a.m.: all reports coming in from the checkpoints are that Ron is doing great. Some rain slowed Ron down on the way to Vermont and the West Virginia checkpoint reported that Ron said he was really glad to see the sun. Ron's sister Carolyn met him at the Maryland checkpoint with a car loaded with food and beverages. Ron wasn't hungry so Carolyn said they had a tailgate party after he left. (He did, however, ride off with a couple of bagels provided by Jackie Mosmiller.)

Day	State	Miles Ridden	Miles to Go
1	10	670	8,128

11 - West Virginia

I recognized Leon Begeman's distinctive "John Deere" Kawasaki as I pulled into the Texaco station in Marlowe. His Ninja 250, the smallest motorcycle of any serious endurance

Leon Begeman
poses with his
"John Deere"
motorcycle
(photo by Leon
Begeman).

riders I know, had been re-painted in the colors of a John Deere
tractor. Now a network engineer, Leon grew up on a farm where
his father owned a dozen or so John Deere tractors. Leon was
the oldest child, so he started out by driving them alongside the
feed bunks while his father threw hay from the wagon. When
asked about the unusual paint job on the motorcycle, Leon
sometimes responds with, "My wife won't let me have a motorcycle. I told her it's a lawn mower."

Leon's motorcycle would be a topic of conversation regard-
less of who was riding it. What makes it even more unusual,
however, is that this diminutive motorcycle belongs to a rider
who stands 6' 3" tall and weighs 155 pounds. When I first met
Leon a year earlier, Abraham Lincoln came to mind. Like our
sixteenth president, Leon has very sharp, definitive features.

Leon and his son Mike are both big guys who have accomplished significant feats on small machines. When Mike was 17,
he became the youngest rider to qualify for membership in the
IBA. He holds the record for the most miles ridden in 24 hours
on a moped. Mike has not only inherited his father's taste in
motor vehicles, but also his physical characteristics too; Mike is

Mike Begeman kneels beside his moped (photo by Leon Begeman).

West Virginia checkpoint: Gary Castleman, John Laurenson, Honey Castleman, Bob Ryan, Ron, Leon Begeman, and Leonard Roy.

5' 11", weighs about 120 pounds, and still has a few years of growing to do.

My West Virginia checkpoint was only 15 miles from Hagerstown, Maryland, the site of the recent Capitol 1000 Endurance Rally. Leon, Leonard Roy, John Laurenson, Mike Sachs, and Gary Castleman participated in the rally. Leon and Mike were planning to witness for me later in the ride, in Virginia and Georgia, respectively.

Day	State	Miles Ridden	Miles to Go
1	11	719	8,079

12 - Pennsylvania
Fellow Iron Butt veteran Fred Johns offered to serve as a witness in either Pennsylvania, Ohio—or both, if I was unable to find other witnesses. In April he had been run off the road by an 18-wheeler and had suffered a minor concussion and several broken bones. Although he wouldn't be able to ride to Pennsyl-

Pennsylvania checkpoint: Bill Koehler, Fred Johns, Ron, and Michael Galloway.

vania, he assured me that he would be available to help me. "I want you to know I *will* be there for you," Fred wrote.

After leaving the checkpoint, I realized that I hadn't asked Fred about his recovery. I hoped he realized I'm not always so insensitive, but was just preoccupied at the time.

Day	State	Miles Ridden	Miles to Go
1	12	792	8,006

After a few minutes, I saw a patrol car following me, checked my speed, and slowed down. As soon as I released the throttle, the trooper pulled me over.

"Oh great," I thought. "Now I'm going to get a speeding ticket for not paying attention. Why didn't I pick this guy up on the radar detector?"

"May I see your driver's license and registration, please?" the officer asked as he approached the motorcycle. "Where are you heading in such a hurry?"

Recalling my successful experience just 12 hours earlier in Massachusetts, I tried the same approach.

"I'm on vacation and I'm just trying to get in some riding," I explained. "I suppose I let the speed get a bit higher than I should have. I don't normally ride that fast," I continued.

"I see you're running a radar detector," the young officer remarked, as he nodded toward the motorcycle. "I don't have to use radar to issue a citation. The law only requires that I pace you for three-tenths of a mile, as I just did. You were running almost 85 mph. Slow down a bit. We won't stop you for going a little over the limit, but you need to be reasonable," he finished, as he returned my license and registration.

"I can't tell you how much I appreciate this, officer. I'll slow it down. Thanks."

When I approached Somerset, I stopped for a brief pit stop at a rest area. As I was preparing to leave, a man walked by on the way back to his car and expressed interest in my motorcycle.

"Where are you heading?" he asked.

I decided to be honest, but brief, and explained that I was in the process of trying to break a record by visiting all 49 North American states.

"Say, what's your name?"

"Ron Ayres."

"Wow, I can't believe this! I've heard about you! A good friend of mine knows you and we were talking about you just the other day. He rides motorcycles too. I just can't believe this. What a coincidence. I'm Allan Gold," the man continued as he extended his hand.

"What's your friend's name," I asked.

Allan hesitated for a moment, then looked embarrassed.

"This is such a surprise, my mind just went blank. And I've known the guy for 25 years."

"That's all right," I offered. "I'm at the age where that happens to me a lot. I've heard it referred to as a 'senior moment.' Where does your friend live?"

"Little Rock," Allan replied, still looking a little flustered and contemplative, as he tried to recall his friend's name.

"Well, you must mean Bill Freeburn or Ken Fisher." I took a stab at the only two riders from Arkansas whose names came immediately to mind, since both would be meeting me in Texarkana in another 40 hours or so.

"That's it! That's it!" Allan responded. "I know both of them! I'm a podiatrist in Little Rock. Here, let me give you one of my cards," Allan continued as he removed his wallet and handed me one of his business cards. "I can't wait until I see them to tell them about this meeting. What a coincidence."

"Well, I'll be seeing both of them soon. They're meeting me in Texarkana."

We talked for a few minutes and I handed him one of my "poop sheets."

Allan studied the map of my route, obviously delighted with the additional details about my ride.

"This is great. Would you mind signing this somewhere?" Allan asked as he handed the sheet to me.

As I signed the sheet, it occurred to me that *I* was now in the position of validating Allan's "poop sheet."

Allan walked to his car, obviously delighted about our chance meeting. Before I left, Allan and his daughter Robin (aka "Bud") returned with a camera to snap a shot of us together by my motorcycle.

Allan, his wife Laura, and Bud had been to Northfield, Massachusetts, where Bud had just graduated with honors from high school. As soon as Allan got back into their vehicle, he called his office and asked them to tell Bill Freeburn about our meeting.

Approximately 20 miles before reaching Pittsburgh, the Pennsylvania Turnpike (I-76) continues to the northwest as I-70 continues west. Because I had picked up I-70 before entering Pennsylvania and followed it to the Pennsylvania Turnpike entrance at Breezewood, I had become accustomed to thinking that I was supposed to stay on I-70, not switch to I-76. When faced with the option of continuing on I-70 or I-76, I opted for the incorrect choice: I-70. For all of the advantages my preprinted route slips afforded me, I wouldn't have made this mistake if I had been using a map rather than the route slips.

I didn't realize I was off-course until I passed the large WELCOME TO WEST VIRGINIA sign, almost 60 miles west of the intersection where I had selected the incorrect route. My plan didn't call for entering West Virginia twice.

I pulled to the shoulder, extracted the map from the trunk and examined my options. I decided to backtrack to Pennsylvania, take a shortcut to get to the Pennsylvania Turnpike north of Pittsburgh, and continue with the original plan. I had been a half-hour ahead of schedule when I reached Pennsylvania, but now I'd be an hour late reaching the Ohio stop.

Although there was more than an hour "buffer" in my schedule, I felt it was particularly important to not fall behind during the first leg. I would have to complete Virginia, Tennessee, North Carolina, and South Carolina between about midnight and 3:30 a.m. Except for the 90-minute nap I had taken in Kittery, I would have been awake for more than 40 hours when I reached Virginia, and nearly 44 hours by the time I reached the motel in South Carolina. Once I left the interstate at Corbin, Kentucky, I would be on dark, unfamiliar secondary roads for 125 miles through the Cumberland Mountains until I connected with I-81 in northeastern Tennessee.

That is, *if* I stayed on schedule. If I arrived in Virginia after the small "Mom and Pop" gasoline station in Ewing closed, it would become a lot worse. I'd have to ride at least an additional 60 miles.

Remembering the importance of making it to the end of this leg on time, I became angry with myself for making the wrong turn in Pennsylvania. It wasn't just that my stupid mistake caused me to fall behind schedule so early in the ride, but I knew that any stress or anxiety would drain my stamina more quickly. Such aggravations would be magnified as I became more tired, something I'd discovered early in my endurance riding career. Even the self-anger I was currently experiencing would consume energy that I should preserve for riding.

As I headed east again, I recalled some classic mistakes other riders and I have made during endurance rallies.

Earlier in the year, Manny Sameiro had published an account on the Internet of the mistakes that resulted in his last place finish in the 1997 Iron Butt Rally. Manny had whimsically titled his account "Against the Pavement," a title apparently inspired by my book *Against the Wind.*

After traveling from Chicago to Madawaska, Maine, during the first leg of the rally, Manny had mistakenly filled his motorcycle with diesel fuel. He discovered the mistake, but replacing the fuel with gasoline, and cleaning the carburetors and fuel lines caused him to fall behind schedule. In an effort to regain the hours lost, Manny pushed his motorcycle beyond its capabilities, lost control, and wrecked his bike. He then purchased the only used motorcycle he could find in the small town of Houlton, Maine, a 1983 Honda VT500 Shadow. Because of the delays he experienced, along with the 10,000 point penalty that was invoked for his having switched motorcycles, Manny finished the rally in last place. I thought Manny deserved a lot of credit for overcoming such difficult obstacles to finish.

When Manny published his account, I sent a message to LDRIDER:

> *Some day I'm going to compile a list of incredibly*
> *dumb things otherwise smart riders have done on the*
> *Iron Butt. I can probably get away with it, since my*
> *own mistakes top the list. It just so happens that*
> *buying diesel fuel isn't on my list yet.*

Shortly thereafter, George Barnes recounted a mistake that he had made, also early in the 1997 Iron Butt Rally. George decided to collect a big bonus by riding to Springfield, Missouri. But he mistakenly headed for Springfield, Illinois. After stopping to sleep in Scranton, Pennsylvania, George caught his mistake, but it was too late to make the trip to the "correct" Springfield.

13 - Ohio

When Brian Mehosky reached the checkpoint near Elyria, Ohio, he discovered there were *two* BP stations in the vicinity of the turnpike exit, and neither of them was easy to find. When Bill Carson and Jerry Flynn arrived, they discussed the situation and agreed that I might have difficulty finding the sta-

Ohio checkpoint: Michael Cox, Brian Mehosky, Ron, William Carson, and Jerry Flynn.

tions. Realizing I was going to exit the turnpike at the toll plaza, the group decided that Jerry and Bill would wait at the turnpike exit to escort me to the BP station. They were soon joined by Michael Cox.

Michael, who works for British Petroleum, was on temporary assignment from Alaska to Cleveland. Michael claims to have traveled the entire 800-mile length of the Dalton Highway from the Pacific port of Valdez to the Arctic Ocean at Prudhoe Bay—60 times!

I had been riding alone since leaving Delaware. Now Jerry Flynn accompanied me to the Michigan checkpoint. It had been exactly twenty hours since I left the Getty station in Kittery, and I had traveled my first 1,000 miles.

Day	State	Miles Ridden	Miles to Go
2	13	1,112	7,686

14 - Michigan

Jim Kraus, Art Holland, Glenn Pancoast, and 1997 Iron Butt veteran Bobb Todd, were among the group that met me at Ottawa Lake. Bobb rode from Toronto to help.

Michigan checkpoint: Jim Kraus, Bobb Todd, Ron, Glenn Pancoast, and Art Holland.

Bobb Todd, Glenn Pancoast, and Ron fill out the necessary
paperwork in Michigan.

Jerry continued riding with me for about 120 miles. I didn't
learn until later that he terminated his ride with me near Sidney, Ohio, after a bus blew a tire and nearly took him down with
it.

Day	State	Miles Ridden	Miles to Go
2	14	1,213	7,585

Leaving Michigan, I now could look forward to a relatively
long route of more than 300 miles through Ohio to Lexington,
Kentucky, via I-75, interrupted by a stop in Lawrenceburg, Indiana. The most convenient way to bypass Cincinnati on my
way south was to take the I-275 loop around the city. I would
briefly cross the state line into Indiana before returning to
Ohio. A stop in Lawrenceburg was like getting a state for free.

It started to get dark as I approached Cincinnati. It was
raining, I was exhausted, and my mood deteriorated quickly. I
glanced at my route sheet and realized that I still had another
450 miles to ride before my first rest stop in South Carolina. I
wondered what ever made me think I was could accomplish
that before my first rest. The deterioration of my mood was emphasized by the mistake I had committed earlier in Pennsylva-

nia, adding both additional miles and additional time to what had already been an ambitious first leg. Worse, the mistake was likely to result in a domino effect, causing me to arrive in Virginia too late to use the planned checkpoint, which would require still more mileage and time before reaching South Carolina for the planned four hours of sleep. The problem would continue into the next leg, and theoretically continue as I fell further behind and lost volunteers due to scheduling problems. The schedule I had developed was very tight with little opportunity to make up lost time. I would have to pay for my mistakes by sleeping even less, or by continuing to arrive late at the checkpoints.

I thought about the embarrassment of having to terminate the attempt so soon. After more than a year of carefully planning an assault on the 48-state record, and after securing the help and good wishes of nearly two hundred friends, I seemed to be blowing the entire thing. This time, I envisioned blowing it because I bit off too much during the first leg, then took a wrong turn from the Pennsylvania Turnpike.

Then again, perhaps the bearings in my front wheel would disintegrate, providing a legitimate excuse to end the ride. After thinking about that possibility for a moment, I decided it would be no less embarrassing for the ride to be terminated because I had foolishly screwed up a new motorcycle merely so I could have shiny wheels. An accident would provide a legitimate excuse to quit, but I wasn't that desperate yet. I wouldn't experience "desperate" until reaching Nevada in another four days.

I knew Mary Sue "Suzy" Johnson would be waiting at Lawrenceburg. Suzy and I became friends after our first Iron Butt Rally in 1995. A truck driver for Roadway Express and a young grandmother, Suzy was the first woman to complete the Iron Butt Rally on a Harley-Davidson. She went on to a fourth-place finish in the 8/48 and finished the 1997 Iron Butt Rally in sixth place.

Thinking about seeing Suzy reminded me of a mutual friend, the late Ron Major. Until his death from a massive coronary during the 1997 Iron Butt Rally, Ron was the only rider

Ron Major and Ron Ayres. Ron Major died of a massive coronary during the 1997 Iron Butt (photo by Suzy Johnson).

who had participated in every endurance event I had entered, including the 8/48.

I recalled how Ron reacted when he saw me waiting for him at the finish of the 8/48, freshly shaven, and in clean clothes. I approached him and offered my congratulations for his first-place finish. He accused me of toying with him.

Ron thought I had finished first and had even had time to shower and change clothes before he arrived. His assumption might have been right if I hadn't lost my receipts in Idaho, but I knew better than to think that way, much less say so. Experienced riders know there are many opportunities for any good ride to go bad. If I hadn't screwed up, I may have struck a deer, or suffered some other mishap.

I assured Ron that he'd won. He found that easier to believe than my story about losing my receipts.

15 - Indiana

I was about an hour late arriving at the Shell station in Lawrenceburg, Indiana. There were more friends awaiting my arrival than I'd expected. In addition to Suzy and Indiana vol-

Ron smiles after being greeted in Lawrenceburg, Indiana (photo by Suzy Johnson).

unteers Stormy Warren and Mitch Comstock, Mike "murf" Murphy and his wife Rena came from St. Louis. Murf, a neurosurgeon with the St. Louis University Health Sciences Center, wasn't planning to be there until a last minute cancellation by one of his patients cleared his schedule for the day. Murf called his wife Rena, asked if she would like to be a part of history, and invited her to accompany him for a 350-mile ride to Lawrenceburg.

As the well-wishers were greeting me, I felt guilty about my recent doubts. The sight of these close friends, who had come so far to simply spend ten minutes supporting my attempt, was more motivating than anything I could have imagined.

Suzy asked me how I was feeling. I admitted that I was very tired, much more so than I had expected to be at this stage of the ride.

"Ron, I've got my van parked right over there," she said, pointing to her vehicle parked beside the service station. "I'm in no hurry to get home. Take a short nap."

"Thanks, Suzy, but I'm already behind schedule and I'm concerned about being able to make the Virginia checkpoint be-

Suzy Johnson gives Ron a "good luck" kiss on the cheek, one of her "famous" hugs, and a couple bananas (photo by Suzy Johnson).

Indiana checkpoint: Michael Murphy, Suzy Johnson, Bob Evans, Ron, Mitch Comstock (with goatee) Rena Murphy, George Herren (in back), and Stormy Warren.

fore the gasoline station closes. As much as I'd love to take a nap, I'd better keep moving."

"Look, I promise I won't let you sleep for more than an hour. Honest. I'll wake you up and get you going again just as soon as you want. You're very welcome to use the van."

It was difficult to pass up the offer. Aside from my reluctance to compromise my schedule even more than I already had, I thought about the large group of supporters who were waiting in Kentucky. I called upon some inner reserve and declined Suzy's generous offer for the final time.

The upcoming 100-mile ride to Lexington, Kentucky, would nail the sixteenth state on my list. As I pulled away from the Shell station, I scolded myself for having had such wimpy and cowardly thoughts less than thirty minutes earlier. How could I even *think* about failing, with so much enthusiastic support from my friends?

Day	State	Miles Ridden	Miles to Go
2	15	1,433	7,365

16 - Kentucky

Christian Dehner coordinated my stop in Kentucky. Christian volunteered to help after his father gave him a signed copy of *Against the Wind* the previous Christmas. Among everyone who volunteered to help, none was more enthusiastic than this eighteen-year-old. He had extracted information about the ride from my web site, prepared briefing materials, and visited with local news stations, encouraging them to cover my arrival.

Shortly before I left Kittery, Christian's mother, Alice, sent me an e-mail message in which she stated that Christian's efforts with the media seemed to be successful, and three stations were planning to be present in Lexington.

As the Chevron station came into view, I saw evidence of Christian's efforts. Several video crews were present with bright floodlights. I dismounted and asked for Christian and the other volunteers, Mark Austin, and Mark Hawkins. After the forms were signed and photographs taken, one of the reporters conducted a short interview about the ride.

Kentucky checkpoint: Mark Hawkins, Mark Austin, Ron, Christian Dehner. Christian played an important role in organizing some local news coverage for Ron's Arrival.

Early the next morning, Gary provided details about the events of the previous evening:

> *Ron arrived about one hour behind schedule after traveling through light rain in Indiana. There were 12 riders and spouses (six on two wheels) on hand with ABC, NBC, CBS, and FOX. Two of the stations did significant pre-arrival backgrounds on the ride and then very nice pieces when Ron arrived.*

> *Christian with his youth and enthusiastic admiration made great copy and regaled the camera crews with Ron's exploits as garnered from Against the Wind.*

> *Ron was remarkably fresh, although he had clearly been up 28 hours or so. He was very gracious with the TV cameras and lights. He was clearly gaining strength from all the well-wishers and stated in the interviews that he "had to make this work now more than ever because of all the support." His actions were deliberate, smooth, and following his routine. So far*

the documentation is intact; the notebook is still cabled to the tail pack!!

When he pulled away, Christian, Mark Austin, and I showed him the way. Once underway any appearance of fatigue disappeared. He took the lead, negotiating traffic and hazards with appropriate changes in speed and lanes. After a dozen miles I decided discretion was the better part of valor (I couldn't keep up). When last seen, he was, like the Pied Piper, leading my 18-year-old son, on his 1983 Honda Nighthawk (CB550SC) off to Virginia, and for all I knew, Alaska.

Gary Dehner

Gary was right. I *did* gain strength from all the well-wishers.

Day	State	Miles Ridden	Miles to Go
2	16	1,519	7,279

17 - Virginia

As I was leaving Lexington, Harold Brooks, E.L. McGuire, and E.L.'s wife, Karen, were arriving at Ewing, Virginia. An hour later, Leon Begeman arrived on his "John Deere" Ninja. Leon, who had also greeted me in West Virginia, was my first "repeat" witness. Although other riders rode with me through several states, Leon was the first to greet me in two states. Leon considered riding with me from the West Virginia checkpoint, but when he learned that I intended to ride nearly 900 miles to get from one to the other, rather than a more direct 435-mile route, he decided to simply meet me in Ewing.

Leon, Harold, and E.L. had all competed in the Capitol 1000. Leon admitted that he had pushed his small motorcycle pretty hard during the rally, and again while heading south on I-81 to Ewing to meet me. The valves on the motorcycle had gotten too tight and the bike wouldn't run at low speed. When he stopped it, the only way he could get it started again was to get it rolling and catch it in gear.

I continued toward Virginia, hoping Harold would be successful in persuading the operator of the gasoline station to remain open until I arrived. Harold has competed in four Iron Butt Rallies and is one of the most well-known, well-liked, and respected riders in the endurance riding community. I knew I could count on him to do whatever was humanly possible to help me. The next few hours would confirm it.

Although I had traveled fewer than 90 miles from Lexington when I exited the interstate highway in Corbin, I stopped to top off my fuel tank. I knew the road through the Cumberland Mountains from Corbin to Ewing would be dark and desolate, and I wasn't sure how soon I would be able to find fuel if Harold hadn't been able to keep the Ewing station open. I didn't want to compound my problems by running out of fuel.

My plan called for riding southeast on Route 25. After crossing the Cumberland Gap, a large, flat area wedged between the Cumberland Mountains, I would ride east on Route 58 to Ewing. If I could purchase gas in Ewing, I would then backtrack about 13 miles to Route 25, then go south to I-81 at White Pine, Tennessee. If the station in Ewing was closed, I would have to continue east to Gate City, Virginia, then try to get back on schedule for North Carolina and Tennessee.

The young man who operated the Exxon station in Ewing planned to close at 10:00 p.m. When Harold explained the situation, the attendant agreed to stay open for another hour, providing his mother would grant him permission. Harold knew I had started from Kittery a half-hour earlier than planned, and the plan called for me to arrive in Ewing by about 10:30 p.m. Harold assured the attendant that I would arrive by at least 11:00 p.m. After phoning his mother, the attendant received permission to remain open for an additional hour.

When I hadn't arrived by 11:45 p.m., Harold headed in my direction, to the top of the mountain, and tried to raise me on the CB. Coincidentally, at that very moment, I was approaching Pinnacle Mountain on the "Skyline Highway" trying to contact Harold. Unfortunately, someone was playing country music on channel 19, making communication impossible. Meanwhile, E.L. called Barbara and learned that I had been delayed.

The attendant's mother ordered her son to close the station and return home immediately. The young man wanted to keep the station open, but reported that his mother feared he was being set up for a robbery.

A few minutes later, I arrived at the dark Exxon station in Ewing where Harold, Leon, E.L., and Karen were waiting. Still mounted on my motorcycle, I tried to use the CB to communicate with Harold. My CB wasn't transmitting, although I could hear Harold and E.L. trying to communicate with me. I pulled beside E.L., who motioned for me to follow him and Harold. Leon followed behind.

Harold had already developed the contingency plan to head for Gate City. He hoped we would find gasoline without having to ride the entire way to Gate City. In the worst case, Harold planned on suggesting that I use Kingsport, located a short distance south of Gate City as the Tennessee checkpoint, and get back on schedule afterward.

Although I was tired, the sight of these friends rejuvenated me. The instant change in pace was invigorating. The stress that I would normally have experienced was ameliorated. I stuck with Harold as we negotiated the occasional twists and turns of the two-lane roads through this desolate area.

Virginia checkpoint: Ron, Harold Brooks, and E.L. McGuire.

Harold's riding proficiency is well known in the endurance riding community. I'm not a slouch, but it wouldn't have surprised me to learn that I couldn't keep up with him on his large Gold Wing. I lost sight of Harold's taillights immediately after leaving Ewing. E.L. was obviously not a novice either, and found myself challenged just to keep up with him and Karen.

Harold is often the recipient of good-natured ribbing from the endurance riding community because of his notable southern accent. I was amused by the CB chatter between E.L. and Harold. During one exchange, I chuckled at how attentive I had to be to understand what they were saying. It reminded me of the challenge I had faced while learning to speak Portuguese several years earlier while living in Brazil.

"How far do you suppose we're gonna have to ride to get Ron some gas?" E.L. asked Harold.

"I don't know exactly. Might be as much as 60 miles to Gate City before we find any."

"I don't know what kind of gas supply Ron's got. I didn't think to ask him when we started off from Ewing," E.L. responded.

I tried again to get through to them on the CB, but to no avail.

I knew I would forget much of the details of this seven-day adventure, but this evening ride would be indelibly etched into my memory for years. It was a beautiful night, the rain had subsided, and I was riding very briskly through beautiful, desolate mountain roads with a small group of friends. There were high-speed sections and some fairly challenging twisty segments, too. I tried to eliminate the stress caused by the uncertainty of not knowing when I would find gas. "What will be, will be," I thought to myself as I tried to remember the words to the popular song, *Que Sera, Sera*. What could be more wonderful than being out here tonight on a road like this one, in the company of such friends? My thoughts were shared by Leon, who later confirmed the significance of the night's ride:

The high point of the weekend was riding on US Route 58 for nearly a hundred miles at 2:00 a.m. with you,

Harold, and E.L. I've told a couple of the sport bikers I
sometimes ride with that it's like getting to scrimmage
with the Red Skins in the new stadium on a Sunday
afternoon. They still think I'm nuts.

As I listened to Harold and E.L. on their CBs, I realized that
they believed it was necessary for me to purchase gasoline in
Virginia. I wanted them to know that a motel receipt would
work just as well, as long as I obtained a receipt showing the
date and time. When we arrived at Duffield, I flashed my lights
and turned into the parking lot of a motel that appeared to be
open.

When E.L. and Karen returned, I explained the situation.

"Harold, Ron's got a solution here. Come on back here to the
motel and let's get this thing sorted out," the CB crackled.

"This will work for us," E.L. continued. "We're about ready
to cash it in for the night anyway, so it might as well be this motel."

"Great," I responded. "I'm looking forward to taking care of
this Virginia situation," I answered.

When Harold returned, I explained that I would pay for a
motel room, use the receipt as proof of having visited Virginia,
then backtrack to pick up with the original schedule. This
would have worked except that the motel was closed and the
manager wouldn't respond to our repeated efforts to wake him.

"Well, what now?" Harold asked.

I was tired and impatient, but knew I should stop and think
before continuing.

"Well Harold, here's the way I see it. If I try to continue all
the way to Gate City, then do the Tennessee, North Carolina,
and South Carolina checkpoints tonight as originally intended,
I'll be so far behind by the time I get four hours of sleep that I'll
screw up the schedule for tomorrow. I hate to stand up the witnesses who are waiting for me tonight, but they're too far away,
now that I've taken this side trip. The best plan now is to forget
those checkpoints, proceed to Gate City, and do Tennessee and
North Carolina the quickest way we can tonight, using you,
E.L., and Leon as witnesses. I'll go to the motel in Greenville tonight as planned and get as much sleep as I can before starting

tomorrow morning on schedule, with a clean slate. Can you guys help me with that?"

"No problem," Harold shot back, without hesitation.

"I'll tell Karen the plan and get on with it," E.L. added as he walked toward the motorcycle, with Karen still perched on the pillion.

"I'll call Barb and let her know what's happening so she can relieve the North Carolina and Tennessee witnesses from duty," I added. I extracted the cellular phone from the tank bag, breathed a sigh of relief when the "roaming" light lit up, and placed the call.

Barbara had home telephone numbers and e-mail addresses for the volunteers, but didn't have a number where she could call them at the checkpoints. I hadn't anticipated the need for *her* to be calling *them.* She sent each of them an e-mail message in hopes that one of them would be able to check it. It was 1:00 a.m. in the east.

As I placed the call to Barbara, E.L. and Karen were having their own conversation.

"He wants to do *what?*" Karen exclaimed, when told about our change in plans.

"Wait a minute," Karen thought to herself, "this night isn't about me and we're not doing it for us. This is about Ron and a special favor we wanted to do for him. He'll be going through a lot more discomfort and inconvenience than we will."

In just a few moments, Karen had talked herself into whatever had to be done over the next several hours.

Leon was preoccupied with keeping his motorcycle running, appearing out of the darkness every now and then like a sprite, ready to follow wherever we would go next. When not cruising through the parking lot where we were holding our planning session, we could hear the distant drone of his motorcycle as he circled the neighborhood to keep the motor going. I looked at my watch and hoped we'd depart the area before some startled neighbors either called the police or shot him.

After reaching Gate City and completing my paperwork, we headed for Kingsport, Tennessee.

Tennessee checkpoint: Ron, Leon Begeman, and Harold Brooks.

Day	State	Miles Ridden	Miles to Go
2	17	1,727	7,071

18 - Tennessee

After signing my witness forms in Tennessee, Leon had had enough of coaxing his motorcycle and decided to spend the night there, intending to visit a repair shop in the morning. Harold, E.L., Karen, and I continued to North Carolina. I was still hoping to finish North Carolina and make it to Greenville for a few hours of sleep before starting the next leg in the morning.

Day	State	Miles Ridden	Miles to Go
2	18	1,731	7,067

The "Volunteer State" volunteers waited nearly eight hours at the checkpoint in Newport. Kelly Council, Principal of Three Oaks Middle School in Dyersburg, Tennessee, rode nearly eight hours to reach the checkpoint and almost lost his prized Aerostich in the process.

When Kelly arrived at the combination convenience store and service station before the other witnesses arrived, he parked under a light about 30 feet from the door of the convenience store. He wouldn't normally leave the suit unattended, but he didn't expect to be far from it. After purchasing a snack, Kelly glanced toward the bike and saw someone dive into the back seat of a car that had been parked next to his motorcycle. As Kelly rushed toward his bike, the car began to drive away. Kelly tried to memorize the license plate number of the car. His Aerostich was gone.

Kelly called the police and filed a report. The officer was friendly, but held little hope the suit would be returned. After running a check of the number Kelly thought he had properly recorded, the officer informed him the number belonged to a GMC pickup truck, rather than to the small, four-door sedan he had seen leaving the parking lot.

When Kelly had arrived at the station, he thought he had seen a young girl with the boys who were driving the car. The young girl had stopped to chat with the cashier of the station, so Kelly thought the cashier might know the girl. He encouraged the cashier to contact the girl to let her know he would not press charges if the suit were returned, and that he knew the license number of the car and would pursue the issue otherwise. He didn't disclose the result of the license number check.

The cashier seemed reluctant to get her friend in trouble, but promised to get in touch with her to report what had happened.

Fifteen minutes later, a car drove to the door of the station. A young lady got out, reached into the back seat, pulled out the Aerostich, and presented it to Kelly, apologizing for her boyfriend as she did so. Kelly thanked her for doing the right thing, then launched into his middle-school principal speech: "If you hang with the wrong crowd you will end up in jail, or dead, and either way your mamma will be crying."

Kelly didn't expect the speech to do any good, but delivering it made him feel better. He later learned that the location had a long-standing history of nefarious behavior. The store was reportedly one of Al Capone's supply points during Prohibition.

Before long, Jim Culp, Don Warren, and Jim's brother-in-law, Geoffrey Greene, joined Kelly. Several hours later, when I was clearly behind schedule, they began to fear the worst. Finally, Don called home to see if there had been any word about my delay. Don's wife Sue was awakened by the call and woke up Matt, their teenage son, who logged onto the Internet. Matt found the message that Barbara had sent a few hours earlier.

"We were starting to imagine the worst," Don later reported. "There was a message from your wife explaining your situation. Praise God for e-mail. All of us Tennessee witnesses cheered when we heard you were still well on your way."

19 - North Carolina

Shortly after crossing the border into North Carolina, I realized I couldn't make it to Greenville without sleep. We had been riding dark mountain roads in the rain for what seemed like hours. The burst of energy that had rejuvenated me upon meeting the group four hours earlier had worn off. I pulled beside Harold at a traffic light in Mars Hill and flipped open my visor.

"Harold, the *only* thing I'm capable of doing at this moment is getting to the nearest motel," I shouted.

"All right. I've been there," Harold responded.

I listened over the radio as Harold notified E.L. and Karen of the plan.

"He needs to stop. Let's pull into the first motel we come to," Harold cracked over the radio.

We pulled into the Comfort Inn in Mars Hill and were relieved that three rooms were available. We decided to sleep for four hours. Then Harold would accompany me to Greenville, and I would try to continue the rest of the ride as close to schedule as possible, starting with Atlanta. The motel's security guard was watching closely as I unloaded my equipment. I explained what I was doing and asked if he would sign my witness form, which he was happy to do.

It was nearly 3:30 a.m. when I reached the room. I hesitated for a moment, deciding whether to take time to shower, or to use the time for a few precious minutes of additional sleep. As eager as I was to close my eyes, I didn't want to wake up in the same sorry condition that I was in. I set the Screaming Meanie, brushed my teeth, jumped into the shower, and hurried to bed. It had been nearly two days since I slept in a bed, and I had 7,000 miles to ride in the next five days.

Day	State	Miles Ridden	Miles to Go
2	19	1,801	6,997

The Screaming Meanie is a small, inexpensive timer designed for truck drivers; it's also used by most endurance riders. Its most distinguishing characteristic is a loud, high-pitched wail that is virtually impossible to sleep through. The device never fails to wake me with a start and initiate a mad scramble to find the "off" switch.

I awoke less than four hours after closing my eyes. The Meanie still had another five minutes to go before its obnoxious wail would sound.

I made a quick call to Barbara so she could inform Wally in South Carolina and alert the volunteers that I would probably be delayed. She posted to the web site:

Tuesday a.m.: schedule delay!!!! *Ron encountered a problem in Virginia in that the checkpoint was not open. He and Harold Brooks went in search of something that was open, but that put him so much off of the route that he could not make the TN, NC, and SC checkpoints as scheduled. In NC they took a motel for about four hours of sleep. Harold will travel with Ron today to Atlanta via SC. They left NC approximately 8 a.m. EST. Ron said he will try to make up as much time as he can today, but he will probably be at least an hour late at each checkpoint and maybe longer. Ron said to offer his apologies to the witnesses in TN, NC, and SC.*

I dressed as quickly as I could, gathered my gear, and headed for the motorcycle. Harold was already standing at his motorcycle examining a map to confirm the most direct route to South Carolina. We decided to ride to Greenville, where I could get on I-85 and continue to Atlanta.

Wally Jordan put a "cop bike" Harley-Davidson tractor seat on a Suzuki and now calls it *Harluki* (photo by Wally Jordan).

Before departing, I tried to fix my radio problem. I suspected a faulty headset cord, as it didn't connect as smoothly as usual. Fortunately, I had a spare cord in my tank bag, so I replaced the faulty cord and tested the transmission again. Harold confirmed that I was transmitting "loud and clear."

As we exited the parking lot, I felt a pang of regret as I thought about the many friends who had so willingly arranged to meet me in Tennessee, North Carolina, and South Carolina. After my ride, I received a message from Iron Butt Rally veteran Hank Rowland. He, Jerry Clemmons, Gregg Garner, LD Holland, and Bryan Moody had waited in North Carolina.

Hi Ron:

I didn't get to see you, 'cuz you were running around with Harold Brooks in Virginia, but I waited with Jerry and a couple of other guys in the wee hours of the morning to see you through North Carolina.

The thing I remember most about that little interlude, besides how it reminded me of other early morning

*stops at gas stations during some long distance effort
or other, is the reaction I got the next day from a co-
worker when I mentioned what I had done the night
before.*

*They were amazed that I would be out at that time of
night, on my motorcycle, "more than 70 miles away
from home." When I tried to explain what you were
doing, they just mumbled into their coffee, wouldn't
even look me in the eye, and walked away.*

*It was a little insight for me of some "normal" folks'
views of the rather extreme nature of the endurance
touring we do at times. Most people don't
understand. . . .*

Best, Hank

Of all of the friends I had stood up in last night's contingent,
I felt the worst about Wally Jordan. Wally was an early volunteer who encouraged me to ask him to go anywhere in the country where I really needed him. Barbara and I first met him in
1996 at the Alberta 2000 Endurance Rally. Wally was 73 then
and took first place over nearly 70 younger competitors including me.

Wally rode almost 2,000 miles from his home in Prescott,
Arizona, to meet me in South Carolina. He waited up all night
for me to check into the motel. Barbara would have called the
motel, but she didn't know Wally had planned to be there with
me. She thought he would be at the checkpoint with other witnesses.

I chuckled as I thought about a snapshot I found while leaf-
ing through a scrapbook in the U.S. Post Office in Madawaska,
Maine, nearly a year earlier when I stopped to collect a large bonus for the Iron Butt Rally. Madawaska is a small town in the
northeast corner of Maine. The town is one of the locations a
rider must visit to qualify for the Four Corners Tour, sponsored
by the Southern California Motorcycle Association. The
Madawaska Post Office maintains scrapbooks with snapshots
of riders who have visited.

The Iron Butt bonus sheet read: "On the fifth sheet count-
ing from the front of the book, beginning with photos from 1992,

is a picture of a bearded man with no name, wearing a red jacket, and standing beside his unusual motorcycle. According to the text beside the picture, what is unusual about his motorcycle?"

When I arrived at the post office and located the snapshot, I recognized the "unidentified" rider as Wally. A notation beneath the snapshot stated that the motorcycle was a combination of a Harley-Davidson and a Suzuki. Wally had named the bike *Harluki*. I later asked Wally about the motorcycle and his Four Corners Tour. Wally wrote:

> *The bike is a 1990 Suzuki DR 650 (single-cylinder, dual-purpose). The Suzuki Motorcycle Company was so impressed that I was able to ride that bike both ways on one trip for the Four Corners run (14,500 miles in 19 total days with a day and a half down time because of snow, at 71 years old), that they gave me a new one.*

> *It was my first attempt at long distance riding . . . and I'm sure I could do it in a much shorter time now that I know more about how much dedication and determination it takes to do that.*

Like many committed endurance riders I have met, Wally has had some very interesting life experiences. Wally once worked on a cruise ship and sailed around the world on 100-day cruises. He was fortunate enough to be able to have his wife accompany him on each of the five such cruises he made.

United States

400 km

0   400 Miles

6

South Carolina to Oklahoma

20 - South Carolina

I followed Harold for 85 miles from Mars Hill to Greenville, South Carolina. I relied on Harold and Lisa Brown, a convenience store clerk, to sign my witness forms.

Day	State	Miles Ridden	Miles to Go
2	20	1,884	6,914

I was euphoric as I headed for Georgia. It was a beautiful, sunny morning, I was rested, and the predicament brought about by my late arrival in Virginia had been resolved. I was looking forward to closing the gap in my schedule, now that I was once again on interstate highways with ideal riding conditions. I assumed that the first leg would be one of the most demanding, and now it was finally over.

As I rode to Georgia, I thought about my incredible good fortune to have friends like Leon, Harold, and E.L. I reflected on the feelings I experienced in the hills of Virginia the night before. There I was with Harold, E.L., and Karen, standing in the rain in a dark, desolate motel parking lot at 1:00 a.m., trying to salvage an ambitious plan that seemed to be unraveling, listening to the high-pitched drone of Leon's motorcycle as he circled the area to keep his vehicle running. I couldn't imagine how I could have come through the night without their help and support. I learned long ago that it's easier to follow an experienced rider than it is to lead the way. After having traveled 1,730 miles during the previous 30 hours, the difference for me was dramatic. From the time I rendezvoused with them at the Exxon station in Virginia, it was as though a significant weight had been removed from my shoulders. I felt very fortunate to have friends who welcomed the opportunity to do whatever they could to assist me.

21 - Georgia

I was still an hour and a half behind schedule when I reached Atlanta, but it was a beautiful morning and I had high hopes of getting back on schedule by the time I reached Florida. Michael Sachs, Gordon Frank, and Dave Lott waited together at the Quick Trip station for nearly two hours before I arrived. Although they had just met, they exchanged stories and discussed motorcycles while they waited.

Mike, my second "repeat witness" had been at the West Virginia stop, but whereas I'd traveled 1,290 miles to get to At-

Georgia checkpoint: Michael Sachs, Ron, Dave Lott, Gordon Frank, and Steve Travis.

lanta from Marlowe, his direct route required a ride of less than half that distance.

As I was having my paperwork filled out, Dave asked me if there was anything else they could do for me. I asked him to call Barbara and ask her to ask my mother to have some fresh bananas available for me when I reached Opelika, Alabama. I removed my Polartec jacket and replaced my clear face shield with the tinted one before leaving the stop.

Gordon reminded me that in Georgia, motorcycles are permitted to use the HOV lane, and traffic moves very briskly through Atlanta on I-85. He offered to ride with me until we were south of Atlanta. Although we were moving noticeably over the speed limit, I was only keeping up with the flow of traffic.

Day	State	Miles Ridden	Miles to Go
2	21	2,009	6,789

22 - Alabama

While I was making my way to Alabama, my mother and her friend Jim Collins were making a trip to a nearby drive-in to buy lunch for Bob Ray, Greg Roberts, and John Harrison, my Opelika volunteers. The volunteers didn't want to leave the station, as they didn't want to miss me when I arrived. My mother lives in Baltimore, but often visits Jim, who lives about 140 miles from Opelika.

As I approached the exit for the Alabama checkpoint, Bob Ray's voice cracked over the CB: "Velcro, are you out there?" Bob asked.

"Bob Ray, is that you I'm listening to?" I replied.

"It's me," Bob responded.

"I've got the exit in sight. I'll see you in 45 seconds or so."

Bob, from Madison, Alabama, competed in the '97 Iron Butt Rally riding a Honda Pacific Coast. He found that the small motorcycle, while reliable enough to make it through the event, wasn't suitable for riding the distances and speeds Bob likes to maintain. He had recently acquired a new Gold Wing.

Alabama checkpoint: Ron, Greg Roberts, Bob Ray, and John Harrison.

As I was refueling, Bob commented that while they were waiting, my mother shared stories about my childhood. Bob stated that he couldn't wait to get on the Internet to share the stories of "Young Ronnie" with my friends.

I thanked my mother for the fresh batch of bananas and ate one before heading to Florida.

Day	State	Miles Ridden	Miles to Go
2	22	2,123	6,675

23 - Florida

I made up almost a half-hour during the 180-mile ride to Century, Florida, arriving only an hour and five minutes behind schedule.

There were several other riders present in addition to my designated witnesses, Jim Boone and Harvey Schneider. Jim rode more than 500 miles from his home in Titusville, Florida, and used the round trip to complete his first 1,000-mile day. He

Florida checkpoint: Tom Wiessner, Corky Reed, Jim Boone, Rebecca Moye, Ron, Harvey Schneider, and Joel Hersh.

rode 1,050 miles in 21 hours, including the time he spent at the Florida checkpoint, to earn his SaddleSore Certificate.

The assembled group included an attractive young woman, Rebecca Moye, from Century. One of the riders told me that Rebecca owned the convenience store and gasoline station. She appeared to be in her mid-twenties.

"Gee, this is exciting," Rebecca gushed as I was preparing the paperwork for signatures. "Nothing like this *ever* happens in Century."

I asked if it was true that she owned the store. When she confirmed that she did, I told her I'd like to introduce her to my unmarried sons.

"Oh, but she's already married," one of the clerks quickly interjected, as if protecting the interests of Rebecca's husband.

"Too bad. I should have assumed as much."

Corky Reed handed me a ticket for the Florida Lottery. "Here, take this. It could be worth $14 million," he grinned. "Just remember who gave it to you if you win."

Ron initiates the paperwork ritual at the Florida checkpoint (photo by Tom Wiessner).

Corky, now nearly 80 years old, lives on a tidal creek on the coast of south Alabama—the "Redneck Riviera." It was a short 65-mile hop for Corky to ride to Century.

A lot of riders stop to visit Corky when they're in the area. One group stopped during a Four Corners Tour, designated the place "Reeds Landing," and bestowed the title of Mayor on him. His retreat was even used as a bonus location in a recent endurance rally.

Although retired since 1980, "Professor" Reed headed a University of Texas radiobiology laboratory at Balcones Research Center in Austin for several years. In the first few years after their retirement, Corky and his wife Joan, who had once been his student, cruised the Caribbean on a sailboat. When she became tired of that lifestyle and wanted to return to teaching anthropology, they had a Mexican standoff. Corky learned to sail the boat by himself and his wife returned to work. They continued to spend vacations and other important events together, but Corky wintered on his sailboat in the Bahamas, and summered on his BMW motorcycle.

In the summer of 1991, Corky and Joan were vacationing together by motorcycle in Alaska, taking a picture of the sign denoting the Arctic Circle. "Corky, we've got to quit meeting this way," Joan said. "If you'll find us some place to live, other than that boat, I'm ready to come back to the coast." Shortly thereafter, they found their place near Perdido Beach and have been living together there happily ever since. Now Corky and his erstwhile student have been together for more than thirty years.

Day	State	Miles Ridden	Miles to Go
2	23	2,304	6,494

24 - Mississippi

Jeff Gordy learned about my ride from LDRIDER and visited the BMW dealership in Hattiesburg where I planned to stop. He arrived at about noon and learned from the owner's son that the local television station was planning to have a reporter

Mississippi checkpoint: Jeff Gordy, Ron, and Melinda Taylor.

available when I arrived. Jeff called Barbara to get an update on my expected arrival time.

When I arrived, Jeff, Melinda Taylor, and a reporter from the local television station were waiting. Melinda's husband Dave had offered to meet me but wasn't able to make it and had arranged for Melinda to be on hand instead. After the paperwork, I spent a few minutes with the television reporter. Then Jeff joined me on my ride to Louisiana, as I began the third day of my ride.

Day	State	Miles Ridden	Miles to Go
3	24	2,512	6,282

We stopped for fuel in Clinton, Mississippi, before continuing across the Mississippi River to Ruston, Louisiana. Jeff rode with me as far as the western bank of "Big Muddy" before returning to his home in Jackson. He called Barb and provided an update when he returned home.

25 - Louisiana

As Louisiana witness Steve Wilson entered the parking lot of the Shell station, a half-dozen people rushed to him, thinking I had arrived. Since Steve had checked the Internet before he left his house five minutes earlier, he was able to give the group an update. Steve, owner of Father and Son Lawn Care in Ruston, typically rides a John Deere 455 all-wheel Steer, 22 hp diesel tractor with a 60 inch deck. On weekends, he switches to his 1995 Honda Pacific Coast 800 motorcycle.

I arrived more than an hour late. The "official" Louisiana contingent included Dan Weber from Shreveport, Dennis Dezendorf from Natchitoches, and Bill Johnson from Leesville.

Dennis, a parole officer and part-time writer for "Interactive Motorcycle," an on-line forum for articles about motorcycling, rode almost 100 miles from his home in Natchitoches with his fourteen-year-old son, Joey. When I dismounted, Joey introduced himself, shook my hand, then proceeded to wet a paper towel and clean the bugs from my headlight.

Louisiana checkpoint: Bill Johnson, Joey Dezendorf, Dennis Dezendorf, Ron with his bananas, Steve Wilson, Dan Weber, and Don Small.

When Joey read in *Against the Wind* about 26-year-old Jesse Pereboom being the youngest rider to complete the Iron Butt Rally, Joey told his dad that the record would only stand until he became old enough to participate in the rally.

While witnesses were completing documentation, others gave *KLONE* a thorough inspection. The tire pressure was checked, the shock absorbers and fork seals were inspected for leaks, and the proper oil level was confirmed. I was also given a fresh batch of bananas.

I considered asking the group to give the front wheel a good shaking to insure that it was still securely attached to the bike, but ultimately opted against it. I knew there was now a lot of Internet traffic about my progress, and decided not to introduce the issue of the front wheel as a topic of concern.

Herb Stark, a colorful, regular contributing member of the Internet BMW Riders Club was eager to escort me to the checkpoint in Texarkana. Herb owns a business that provides advertizing on lighted billboards. He also owns a blueberry farm and a motorcycle campground in Avinger, Texas. Jack West, a rider from Shreveport, rode to Texarkana with us.

Day	State	Miles Ridden	Miles to Go
3	25	2,747	6,051

26 - Arkansas

The late-night ride from Louisiana to Texarkana was another great opportunity to enjoy riding under the full moon, escorted by riders familiar with the territory.

I was looking forward to surprising Ken Fisher and Bill Freeburn with the story of my coincidental meeting with their friend, Allan Gold, in Pennsylvania. "You guys are never going to believe who I met the other day," I proclaimed, as I removed my helmet and earplugs.

"You met Allan Gold," Bill replied. "He was so excited about meeting you that he called from the road to tell me about it."

Arkansas checkpoint: Bill Freeburn, Ron, and Ken Fisher.

"Damn!" I responded. "I've been looking forward to surprising you guys for the last 2,000 miles, and he's gone and taken the fun out of it."

My Arkansas and Texas checkpoints were across the street from each other. I could literally have pushed the motorcycle across State Line Avenue to get from Arkansas to Texas.

Despite Herb's best efforts to help me make up time, I was still an hour late when I reached Texarkana. My plan called for me to ride hard between checkpoints and to spend only ten minutes at each. Except for the four designated motel stops, the schedule called for constant movement. Since the Arkansas and Texas stops were close together, I hoped to keep the two stops to fifteen minutes so that I could pick up five minutes between them.

Day	State	Miles Ridden	Miles to Go
3	26	2,885	5,913

27 - Texas

The last time I talked to Barbara, I had asked her to alert Randell Hendricks, one of my Texas witnesses, that the backrest on my trunk box was coming loose. Randell walked to the Arkansas checkpoint from Texas to get a head start on the repair, then walked back again as I rode the bike to Texas.

Although Randell was a relatively new member of the Iron Butt Association, he had established some solid credentials in a short time. One of the endurance rides sponsored by the IBA is the 50cc, which requires that a rider travel from one coast of the United States to the other in less than 50 hours. At the same time I was riding the 1997 Iron Butt Rally, Randell raised the "coast-to-coast" bar by being the first rider to perform a 100cc. Randell rode from Jacksonville, Florida, to San Diego and back in less than 100 hours.

To celebrate his indoctrination into the Iron Butt Association, Randell had the IBA logo tattooed on his left arm. In recognition of his display of enthusiasm for endurance riding, Mike Kneebone bestowed a coveted honor upon him. Randell forwarded Mike's e-mail message to me:

Texas checkpoint: Dan Vanlandingham, Ron, Eddie Metz, and Randell Hendricks.

. . . in honor of your IBA tattoo, you will be Rider #1 on the 1999 Iron Butt Rally starting line. I signed your 100cc Insanity Certificate today. It should be mailed on Monday.

Eddie Metz and Dan Vanlandingham were my other Texas witnesses. Eddie was a high-placing finisher in the '93 and '95 Iron Butt Rallies. Dan, like Phil Urbanek who had volunteered to meet me in Illinois, was a fellow executive with EDS. I had come to know him the previous year during a company-sponsored executive development program at Babson College in Boston. A relatively new rider, Dan rode to Texarkana from his home in Houston on a rather small 600cc Kawasaki motorcycle. It was the farthest Dan had ever ridden.

Randell handed me a copy of an e-mail message that Mike Kneebone asked Randell to relay to me in Texarkana:

Make sure you tell Ron not to let being behind the curve get to him. Please let him know that I said Fran and I floated all over our "plan." At one point we were behind the plan by more than 14 hours after I got an eye infection, then we hit bad weather, road closure (a

*plane on the road, the highway patrol closed the road
and would not let us by, and no other roads close by),
and my bike broke. However, we made good time in
other places and so will he.*

In addition to the witnesses, several other friends came to
Texarkana, including Jack Tollett, Rallymaster of the Waltz
Across Texas Endurance Rally, and Vince Putt, who works for
the CBS affiliate station in Dallas. Vince brought video equipment to shoot some footage of my arrival for the evening news.

Norm Grills from the Lone Star BMW Riders Club in Dallas
decided at the last minute to show up.

"I was sitting in the den at about 8:00 p.m. after getting the
latest update on Ron's progress when I said to Sandy, 'I sure
would love to be in Texarkana when Ron rolls through,'" Norm
said. "Much to my surprise, she said 'Then go!' Fifteen minutes
later I was heading out of the driveway."

While I was setting out through northeastern Oklahoma,
Texarkana witness Dan Vanlandingham was in a motel room
adjacent to the Texarkana checkpoint, contemplating the large
blister that had developed on his butt during his ride from
Houston. Dan considered getting up to check *it* out in the mirror, then decided he didn't really want to see how bad it was.

"The thing felt as large as an orange," Dan reported. "I was
afraid that if I got up and actually looked at it, there would be
no way I'd get back on the bike in the morning. How in the
world am I ever going to ride all the way back to Houston with
this problem," he thought.

Day	State	Miles Ridden	Miles to Go
3	27	2,886	5,912

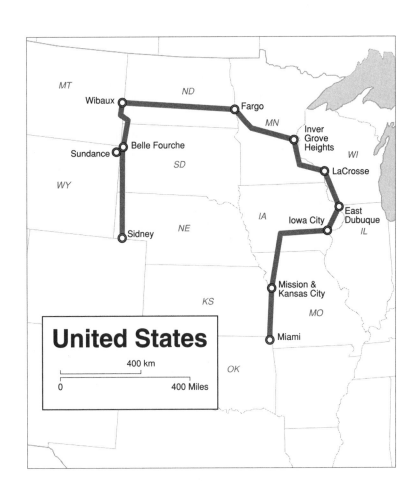

United States

400 km

0   400 Miles

7

Oklahoma to Nebraska

---

28 - Oklahoma

A few weeks before the start of my ride, I changed the
Oklahoma checkpoint from Miami to Broken Bow. I originally
planned to arrive in Miami at 4:50 a.m. to check into a motel.
Iron Butt Rally veterans Ardys Kellerman and Boyd Young
were to meet me when I awoke four hours later.

I knew I could count on Ardys and Boyd to show up wherever I asked, but I didn't see any point in asking them to go to
Miami when I would pass through Broken Bow hours earlier.
The change would reduce Boyd's travel by about 100 miles, and
would be almost 200 miles shorter for Ardys.

Ardys rode 350 miles from Lexington, Texas. A grandmother in her sixties, Ardys has competed in three Iron Butt
Rallies and has been a top finisher in the annual BMW Motorcycle Owners Association high-mileage contests. Boyd, a veteran of the '95 and '97 rallies, rode almost 100 miles from
Atoka, Oklahoma, accompanied by his son and his father.

Although I changed the location of the Oklahoma checkpoint, I still planned to use the original route and the motel
room in Miami. I studied the route between Broken Bow and
Kansas City and considered changing to a more direct route. At
the last moment, I retained the Miami alternative, since it did-
n't seem that the shorter, more direct route would save time.

Ardys knew where Broken Bow was. She and I passed it
while riding back to Texas together after participating in the

Oklahoma checkpoint: Ardys Kellerman, Boyd's son Sam, Boyd
Young, Ron, and Sam Young.

Kansas City Steak Run. I had used the ride as an excuse to introduce her to the beautiful, twisty Talimena Scenic Drive.

I pushed the speed a little between Texarkana and Broken
Bow, as I was familiar with the route and knew it was unlikely
the highway would be patrolled at this time of night. By the
time I arrived at 1:50 a.m., I had made up all but twenty minutes of the gap in my schedule.

I asked Boyd about the weather I should expect on the way
to Miami.

"There were thunderstorms north of here a little earlier
this evening, but they should have blown over by now," Boyd
promised.

That may have been true, but I was about to encounter a
new series of localized storms on my way north.

I enjoyed meeting with these friends, but after talking with
them for a few minutes, Ardys reminded me that I didn't have
time for this, and should get moving. I appreciated her reaction,
but her comment took me a little by surprise. It was the first

time anyone had suggested I was lingering too long at a check-point!

Day	State	Miles Ridden	Miles to Go
3	28	2,961	5,837

Route 259 north from Broken Bow is a two-lane highway through the Ouachita Mountains of southeastern Oklahoma. I expected to make good time at this hour of the morning, as there would be little traffic. I couldn't recall ever seeing the highway patrolled, even during the day.

Leaving Broken Bow, Route 259 is a fast, straight highway for about 50 miles before it begins its ascent into the Ouachita Mountains. As I began climbing and the road changed to a twistier one, I encountered rain and heavy fog. To stay on the road, I had to open my face shield, reduce my speed to about 20 mph, and carefully observe the white fog line that marked the shoulder. I was more concerned about being overtaken from behind than of overtaking another vehicle. Also, I had encountered deer many times before in this area, and I wondered whether they were more or less likely to be on the road in conditions such as these.

I finally descended the north side of the Ouachita Mountains. The rain stopped, the fog dissipated, and I picked up the pace as I turned on to Route 59 toward Sallisaw.

The 130-mile ride from Broken Bow to Sallisaw had required almost three hours. When I approached Sallisaw, a storm to the west looked even more threatening than the one I had just been through. The rain had stopped, but I saw a lot of lightning. Miami was still 130 miles away. I could almost feel the storm moving to the east. If I continued, I would certainly have to ride through it. I decided to take a motel room in Sallisaw instead.

I quickly showered, brushed my teeth, and set the Screaming Meanie to sound in three and a half hours. When I awoke at 8:15 a.m., I consulted the maps to see if it made sense to continue along the original route to Miami, as I no longer planned to use the motel there.

I decided to eliminate the unnecessary trip, and headed for Route 71, about 25 miles to the east. Returning to Texas from the Kansas City Steak Run a few months earlier, Ardys Kellerman and I had taken Route 71 south from Kansas City to Mena, Arkansas. I thought that much of the route was a good four-lane highway that was as fast as an interstate. I called Barbara to file my report for the web site:

> *Wednesday 8:15 a.m.: Ron called from a motel on I-40 about 160 miles from KC. He was loading up the bike and getting ready to head out after about three hours sleep. He sounded in great spirits and said he had some interesting stories to tell about all the help he has been given. He expects to be close to on-time for the beginning checkpoints today.*

In retrospect, I lost time as a result of this change in plans. Route 71 was a twisty, two-lane rural route for 75 miles through the Boston Mountains from Alma, Arkansas, to Bentonville. It was punctuated by an occasional construction zone, traffic accident, or extended ride behind slow-moving eighteen-wheelers in no-passing zones. It wasn't until I reached the Ozark Plateau in southern Missouri that I could resume highway speeds.

The 340-mile ride from Sallisaw to Kansas City was all the more aggravating because of malfunctioning turn signals. My right turn signal blinked constantly, even when I selected the left one. To reduce confusion caused by the errant signal, I depressed the hazard warning indicator, which caused both the left and right signals to flash. At least this wouldn't confuse drivers by causing them to anticipate a turn I didn't intend to make.

I stopped to refuel in Lamar, Missouri, and called Barb to report that my hopes for beginning the day's checkpoints on time had been shattered once again.

29 - Kansas

I was nearly two hours late arriving at the Kansas checkpoint. Thirty minutes after I was due in Missouri, Paul Glaves rode twelve miles to the Kansas checkpoint, called Barbara, and learned of the morning's delays. When I entered the parking lot

Kansas checkpoint: Charles Purvis, Ron, and Lloyd Forester.

of the Quick Trip in Kansas City, Paul headed back to Missouri to wait for me. Charles Purvis and Lloyd Forester were on hand to sign my paperwork.

A week before my ride began, Lloyd, a Kansas City dentist, had canceled 32 appointments and granted his employees a day off with pay so he could perform witness duty and ride with me. After refueling and performing the customary paperwork, Lloyd led the way to the Missouri checkpoint. I was looking forward to seeing the three friends who had volunteered to be in Missouri.

Day	State	Miles Ridden	Miles to Go
3	29	3,422	5,376

30 - Missouri

As I exited the ramp from the interstate highway, I was greeted by the sight of an attractive blonde in red leathers waving enthusiastically as I approached. Red is Voni Glave's trademark color: Red leathers, red boots, red helmet, red bike, red everything. Even the car she almost never drives is red. Voni and her husband Paul are well-known motorcycling enthusiasts who

Missouri checkpoint: Voni Glaves, Scott Young, Ron, and Paul Glaves.

currently own eight BMWs. Paul describes their passion as a hobby run amok.

Voni has ridden 400,000 miles on her BMWs in the past fifteen years. In the BMW Motorcycle Owners of America annual mileage contest, she has been the first-place female rider four out of the past seven years, and the last three years in a row. In the past ten years she has racked up the highest cumulative mileage in the contests—with more than 290,000 miles, which accounts for only six months of each year. Paul claims that Voni's favorite motorcycle, a red 1994 R1100RS with 186,000 miles on the odometer, is the highest-mileage R1100 in the United States. And they are all Voni's miles.

Voni is a special education teacher who works with high school students with learning problems. The fact that she rides her motorcycle to school almost every day has made her somewhat of a folk hero among the students.

When Voni and Paul arrived at the Texaco station, Voni explained what was going on to the manager so he wouldn't be concerned about all of the activity at the pumps. Far from being concerned, he was excited about the event. He provided free bottled water and offered to block a gas pump with trash cans so I wouldn't be delayed.

Several weeks before my ride, Voni had written to wish me well and asked if Paul could do anything for me during my stop in Missouri. She stated that he would be happy to check out the motorcycle while I refueled and completed paperwork for the stop.

"Thanks anyway, Voni," I wrote in response. "I appreciate the offer, but I think I'll be in real trouble if I need Paul's help at that point in the ride."

Famous last words. Now I was grateful for someone with Paul's expertise.

Paul is a member of the Board of Directors of BMW MOA and is the Technical Editor of the BMW Owners News. He conducts "Fix Your Bike" seminars in the spring for the Kansas City and Topeka BMW clubs, and presents technical seminars at the BMW MOA National Rally. When he isn't riding, Paul is the Community Development Director for the city of Merriam, Kansas, a suburb of Kansas City. Paul is entered in the 1999 Iron Butt Rally and plans to use his 1986 BMW K75 which he bought new, and which now has 250,000 miles on the odometer.

I removed my helmet and earplugs and quickly described the problem with the turn signals. Paul immediately went to work. He thought the problem was caused by moisture shorting the turn signal switch on the handlebar, or the relay socket in the electrical box under the fuel tank. Since the switch was easier to get to and more exposed to the rain, he began disassembling it. As Paul opened the mechanism, the manager of the station ran back into the station, and returned with a can of WD-40 to assist with the repair. Paul sprayed the contact area and worked the switch a few times, but the problem persisted. Then Paul saw the source of the problem.

Two wires to the turn signal switch are soldered onto connectors on the back of the switch. The two soldered connections were so close together, however, that they were almost touching. Any moisture between these wires would conduct from the hot wire to the ground wire—just as if the switch were on. Paul turned off the key and used a penknife to separate the connections slightly. By the time I refueled and had secured the signatures on the witness forms, Paul had reassembled the turn signal mechanism.

"What an adventure," I declared as Paul was finishing the repair.

"Thanks for sharing it with us," Voni remarked.

After the surprising turnout in so many of the 30 states I had now visited, I was beginning to understand that many riders were appreciative of the opportunity my ride was providing for them to participate. Many were participating vicariously on the Internet, while several hundred more were either helping as witnesses, riding with me for part of the trip, or showing up at checkpoints to provide moral support.

Scott Young was also one of my witnesses in Missouri. A policeman, former Harley-mounted motor cop, firearms instructor, and sniper/observer for a tactical team, Scott was one of my first friends to volunteer. I met Scott in the spring of 1997 at the Kansas City Steak Run, which attracted a few dozen endurance riders from around the country. Later that year, Scott and about 75 other long-distance enthusiasts attended a barbecue at my home. By the time Scott arrived, my garage, driveway, and backyard were packed with motorcycles. After having seen the way Scott handled his large police bike, and knowing something about the typical riding skills of motorcycle police officers, I suggested that Scott park his bike in a particularly difficult-to-reach spot in the corner of my yard. Without hesitation, Scott deftly maneuvered into the designated niche between several trees, causing several people to comment on his impressive "grand entrance."

As we left the service station, Lloyd took the lead to escort me to Iowa. Voni accompanied us for awhile.

Day	State	Miles Ridden	Miles to Go
3	30	3,435	5,363

Iowa checkpoint: Ken Lefler, Jeff Lambert, Ron, Pam Dempster, Kerry Willey, and Brad Hogue.

31 - Iowa

Pam Dempster, a director of the BMW Motorcycle Owners Association, recommended that we meet at the Hawk-I Truck Stop in Iowa City. I had managed to make up more than an hour of lost time and arrived at the checkpoint only about thirty minutes behind schedule. Ken Lefler and Jeff Lambert were also there to greet me. Among the other friends who turned out was Iron Butt Rally veteran Kerry Willey.

A week earlier, Jeff Lambert had ridden my route from the Iowa to the Illinois checkpoints and he now offered to escort me through the rural Iowa and Illinois countryside. I kidded Jeff about this being his opportunity to pay me back for having led him astray during the '97 Iron Butt Rally. We had been riding together as we approached San Francisco and Jeff asked if I knew the way through the city to the Golden Gate Bridge. Believing I did, I took the lead and proceeded to get us lost. It was the only instance during the rally when I had to stop and ask for directions.

A veteran rider who has logged more than 500,000 miles on motorcycles during the last 35 years, Jeff has ridden in all of the lower 48 states. I was delighted that he led the way for the 85-mile ride from Iowa City to East Dubuque. It gave me the opportunity to notice the lovely weather. The temperature was about 75 degrees, it was sunny, and there was no wind.

Day	State	Miles Ridden	Miles to Go
4	31	3,733	5,065

32 - Illinois

As a crowd awaited my arrival in East Dubuque, Mike Pecora was interviewing the riders to create a video of the event. Mike Cornett, winner of the 1997 Minnesota 1000 Endurance Rally and a fellow participant in the '96 Utah 1088 Rally, was among the familiar faces there to greet me. Mike has collected more than 350 National Park Stamps as a result of doing the Iron Butt Association National Parks Tours. He's visited more parks

Illinois checkpoint: Evan Shockey, Kim Shockey, Joan Oswald, Mike Cornett, Ron, Phil Urbanek, Todd Zedak, Ann Marie Hickey, and Mike Pecora.

than any other rider I know. A professor of communications at Loyola University, Mike had ridden from Chicago to see me.

"When I was in Texas last year, Ron rode almost 250 miles from Plano to Bee Cave to have lunch with me and several other riders," Mike reported. "The least I could do was ride 185 miles from Chicago to wish him well as he came through."

Before I arrived, Kim Shockey had reserved the restroom key to insure that I would be able to make a pit stop without having to wait. When I pulled up to the pumps, Kim's eleven-year-old son Evan approached with a dripping wet squeegee and began to scrape the bugs from my windshield. Evan was already a decent motorcyclist in his own right, at least on dirt bikes. The boy owns an old XL250 and performs his own routine maintenance.

On previous stops, volunteers, including young children, had asked if I would like to have them clean my windshield. In each case, I politely refused the offer, as service station squeegees will sometimes scratch the surface of the windshield, and the thick mess of spattered bugs and dirt on the windshield were no detriment to my visibility, as I ride with the windshield low enough to look over it, not through it.

Evan was eager to help, however, even glancing up to see that I approved of the job. I didn't have the heart to embarrass him by refusing his help or suggesting he had done something wrong. Instead, I thanked him and watched as he scraped enthusiastically at the imbedded dirt and bugs. Meanwhile, Todd Zedak opened my water reservoir and filled it with cold water.

I purchased a sandwich and a V-8, hastily gobbled the sandwich at the pump, and made a quick pit stop. Before leaving, I changed the face shield on my helmet from the dark, smoke-colored shield I prefer in the daytime to the clear shield I use after dark. I can usually perform the change in a relatively short time, but I found myself struggling to get the shield aligned properly as I attempted to secure it to the helmet. I recognized this as a warning sign that I was becoming fatigued and made a mental note to try to be especially careful. After several minutes, I was finally able to get the clear shield installed properly.

My EDS co-worker Phil Urbanek volunteered to meet me in Illinois. I was especially grateful for his support because I knew that Phil, an avid sports fan, was passing up an opportunity to see the big basketball game between the Chicago Bulls and the New Orleans Jazz.

Joan Oswald, who had recently become so interested in endurance riding that she competed in the '97 Iron Butt Rally, wanted to be a witness but also wanted to attend the Harley-Davidson 95th Anniversary celebration in Milwaukee with her son Alex and her husband Rick. Rick suggested that Joan greet me in Illinois, then head to Milwaukee. Instead, she detoured with me to Wisconsin and Minnesota before heading for Milwaukee.

Before departing, I autographed several copies of *Against the Wind*. Ann Marie Hickey had won a copy of the book at a motorcycle rally. She had been given a choice of several prizes and selected the book, to the dismay of her "significant other" who thought she should have selected a prize with a higher monetary value. Specifically, he had wanted her to choose a bike lock. But Ann Marie wanted her own copy of my book, knowing she would have the opportunity to have it autographed in Illinois.

Todd Zedak, who had received a speeding ticket on his way to meet me, offered to lead the way toward La Crosse. Joan, Mike Pecora, Jeff Lambert and I rounded out the quintet as we enjoyed some very nice rural roads along the way.

Immediately after exiting the parking lot, Mike Pecora began blowing his horn to attract my attention. I knew immediately that he was trying to notify me that I hadn't secured the lid to the top case. I stopped, rectified the problem, thanked Mike for bringing it to my attention, and continued toward Wisconsin. So soon after the difficulty replacing my face shield, the need to ride carefully was reinforced yet again.

After about 80 miles, Todd and Mike waved goodbye and headed home to Chicago.

Day	State	Miles Ridden	Miles to Go
4	32	3,818	4,980

Wisconsin checkpoint: Jeff Dean, Ron, Joan Oswald, and Debbie
Forbes.

33 - Wisconsin

As we approached the Kwik Trip Convenience Center in La
Crosse, Jeff Dean and Debbie Forbes were sitting at a picnic ta-
ble with their motorcycles parked nearby. Although I had never
met either of them, I recognized Jeff, the president of the BMW
Motorcycle Owners Association, from photographs in BMW ON
(BMW Owners News).

My escort, Jeff Lambert, didn't recognize the checkpoint
right away, and he continued on for a block or so before realizing
his oversight and returning to the station. I stopped and parked
at the pumps. Joan pulled to the pump next to me, dismounted
and walked with me to greet Jeff and Debbie.

"How far is I-90?" I asked, as Jeff rose.

"About a half-mile that way," Jeff responded, pointing in
the direction of the highway.

"Then this must be the place," I responded.

"That depends on what you're here for."

"I'm Ron Ayres," I replied, extending my hand.

"But you don't look that tired," Jeff laughed.

As I was refueling, Jeff asked me to sign his copy of *Against the Wind*.

In the August 1998 issue of BMW ON, Jeff wrote an article about our meeting in Wisconsin. In it, Jeff wrote of me: "Smiling broadly, [Ron] confessed to being a 'gabber.' He likes to talk and therefore rarely leaves within the ten-minute window he allows for checkpoint stops."

After reading the article, Barbara and my youngest son Brad kidded me about Jeff's observation. At home, I'm usually accused of being too quiet. My sons have often teased me about how difficult it is to engage me in conversation. As I told Jeff, I was spending more time than I intended at checkpoints because I was enjoying the opportunity to meet so many old friends and new acquaintances. Although the witnesses understood my need to keep moving, I hated to appear disinterested in visiting with them, after they had made personal sacrifices to be present.

Joan had planned to accompany me to the Minnesota checkpoint before heading for Milwaukee. Although it was only about 210 miles from La Crosse to Milwaukee, making the trip via the Minnesota checkpoint would add another 250 miles to her ride. And she would be leaving Minnesota after midnight.

I suggested that she might not be comfortable riding her Harley as briskly as I intended on the stretch of interstate between La Crosse and Minnesota.

"It won't be a problem," Joan assured me. "Besides, you don't ride much faster than I normally do."

By the time Joan, Jeff, and I would reach the next checkpoint, I would regret questioning her riding ability or her stamina.

Day	State	Miles Ridden	Miles to Go
4	33	3,942	4,856

It was a beautiful night, illuminated by a full moon with clear skies, and the ride to Minnesota was scheduled to take about two hours. Before an hour had passed, drowsiness was beginning to set in, and I recognized one of endurance riding's most important warning signs: I began to have difficulty maintaining a constant speed. Just as I was becoming concerned, I was startled by the sound of Joan's loud exhaust pipes as she passed.

Joan knew about a speed trap at Coates, Minnesota. She also noticed that I had drifted over the centerline a few times and thought that if she passed me she would possibly wake me and alert me to the speed trap. As she passed, I was so startled that I received a shot of adrenaline that sustained me until the Minnesota checkpoint. I've never agreed with the "loud pipes save lives" philosophy, but on this occasion, I appreciated their effect. Thanks, Joan.

34 - Minnesota

Pete Dean had suggested the Conoco truck stop at Inver Grove Heights for the Minnesota checkpoint. He knew I would be arriving after dark and felt that the large oil refinery located a few miles south of the station would be an excellent landmark. As I approached the refinery, I thought about the stark contrast between the daytime and nighttime appearance of things. During the day, refineries look nasty and offensive. At night, they look like starry clusters, with beautiful, twinkling lights.

The refinery reminded me of my visits to Venezuela. The first time I entered Caracas, it was nearly midnight on a December evening and the route to the city from the airport made its way through the foothills of the beautiful Andes Mountains. The thousands of lights blanketing the mountain were so beautiful that I thought it had been decorated for Christmas. During the day, I saw that the beauty of the mountains was scarred by thousands of makeshift slums inhabited primarily by the impoverished masses and refugees from Caribbean countries. Their hovels had neither electricity nor plumbing, so electricity was "pirated" by illegally tapping into the power lines from the highway. The uncovered, solitary bulbs used to light the dwellings had transformed the daytime visage of a slum to a Christmas garden at night.

A week before my scheduled arrival, Pete learned there was highway construction on I-494. He test-rode the route the day before my arrival and decided there would not be a problem at the time of night I would be arriving. Pete's check was so thorough that he purchased fuel at the Conoco station and learned that the time stamp was off by fifteen minutes. When he pointed this out to the clerks who were on duty, they were excited to learn that something so important would be happening at their station, but told Pete he would have to come back and discuss the problem with the manager of the station during the daytime. Pete did so, and the time was corrected before my arrival.

Pete arrived at the checkpoint an hour before my anticipated arrival to be certain he would be present if I was early. By midnight another seven or eight riders had filtered in.

Loren Sullivan rode to Minnesota from Plano, Texas. A member of the Lone Star BMW Riders Club in Plano, Loren had attended a club dinner a few months earlier at which I had been a guest speaker. I had talked primarily about my participation in the '95 and '97 Iron Butt Rallies, but finished with a description of my upcoming 49-state ride. This interested the riders as much as my Iron Butt experiences. A few days after the dinner, I received an e-mail message from Loren in which he volunteered to ride to Minnesota to be a witness, after having noticed on my Internet home page that there were only two other witnesses identified for that state.

By about 12:25 a.m., the waiting riders heard the distinctive sound of an approaching Harley-Davidson, soon to be followed by Joan's announcing, "He's right behind me."

By the time I reached Minnesota, word had spread far and wide on the Internet that I was eating a lot of bananas, so Pete had a fresh bunch available. Although I still had a supply in my top case, they were becoming pretty soft, so I exchanged some of my "wilted" ones for the fresh ones that Pete had brought. I ate one as I was getting witness forms signed.

Pete later wrote:

Minnesota checkpoint: Loren Sullivan, Roger Ries (with glasses), John Herman, Jeff Lambert, Ron, Brent Bruns, Joan Oswald, (unidentified), and Pete Dean.

When you got off your bike you were moving pretty slowly. You looked very tired. I was amazed that you could remember the names of the checkpoint people. You asked for Loren and me by name. When I'm that tired I can't even remember my own name.

As I was refueling, Brent Bruns noticed that my CB antenna was short by about two feet. Brent had completed a SaddleSore ride just a month earlier to qualify as an IBA member. He quickly tried to swap the antenna from his new Gold Wing, but it didn't fit. Instead, he offered to get word to the Washington checkpoint, where I was planning to have the motorcycle serviced, to have a replacement on hand.

Before leaving the checkpoint, Scott Ward joined me for the ride through North Dakota, Montana, South Dakota, and Wyoming. Scott had recently purchased an "endurance rally-equipped" Honda ST1100 from Don Moses and was eager to use it to earn his SaddleSore 1000 certificate. The ST1100 was equipped with a CB radio, and I was looking forward to chatting with another rider. We tested my radio to insure that it would function at close range.

Scott Ward joins Ron's quest at the Minnesota checkpoint (photo by Scott Ward).

"Do you mind chatting on the CB while we ride, or would you prefer not to be bothered?" Scott asked.

"I'd like the change."

"Good, because there are a lot of things I'd like to ask you."

As I was preparing to leave the checkpoint, I thanked Joan for her escort. After riding more than 550 miles from her home to my Illinois and Wisconsin checkpoints, she was now less than ten miles from her home. But she was preparing to ride to Milwaukee to join her family.

I had expected Jeff Lambert to return home after riding to Minnesota, but he appeared to be ready to keep riding. I asked if he was planning to continue to Fargo.

"Oh sure, why not?" Jeff replied. Jeff figured that since he couldn't make it home in time to be at work in another six hours, he might as well ride to Fargo. Fortunately, he only had his father to answer to, as they own an automobile body shop. Before leaving Minnesota, Jeff asked Scott's wife to call his wife Dianna to let her know of his plan to continue to North Dakota.

Day	State	Miles Ridden	Miles to Go
4	34	4,076	4,722

There were five others riding with me as I left the checkpoint, but two dropped off almost right away. On the other hand, Pete Dean originally intended to accompany me for just a few miles, but became so captivated with the excitement that he rode farther than he had intended.

The pack was traveling fast. I don't like traveling faster than 80 mph, and within two miles everyone was pulling away. The road split. Whoever was leading knew the way and took the branch I would have suggested. One branch goes to St. Paul and the other to Minneapolis. Both branches intersect with I-494. The Minneapolis branch is shorter but has seven sets of traffic lights. The pack of riders took the St. Paul branch. I took the Minneapolis branch.

I regretted my decision immediately. Here was one of the biggest adventures I would ever be involved in, and I let my participation die because I wouldn't go faster than 80 mph. My only hope now was to run the gauntlet of lights on roads with a 50 mph limit and head 'em off at the pass. I pushed hard. Real hard. I think I may have even stretched the speed limit a bit. There were only two lights that slowed me down, but when I got to I-494, the road was empty.

I slowed my pace, reasoning that if you had already passed I would never catch up but if you were behind me, I would be overtaken soon. As the miles passed I started to resign myself to being left behind. I started composing an e-mail in my head that I could post to the list of volunteers. If I couldn't have fun, I could at least be useful.

Then, three miles from my workplace, where I would have stopped to send the e-mail, Scott Ward passed me. The whole pack passed and you gave me a wave as you went by. Well, that was it. I decided there would be no e-mail that night and I would not be left behind. I attached myself to the back of the formation and took a ride. At the junction of I-494 and I-94 two riders peeled away. That put me two riders behind you. Then after about 20 more miles you shifted back a position and I was right behind you.

The night was cool. There was a full moon, little wind,
and no bugs. It was a great night for a ride.

I noticed you were letting your feet dangle below the
foot pegs and was reminded how tired you must be.
Soon time and distance began to weigh on me. I had
an 8:00 a.m. meeting the next day. At the first St.
Cloud exit I pulled what must have been a very
graceless loop around you and waved as I exited. If
nothing else, it reminded you to stay alert.

As we approached Sauk Centre, Minnesota, I expected to encounter a storm. Looking to the northwest, bright flashes of lightning were illuminating massive, swollen cumulonimbus clouds. I had traveled about 130 miles since refueling at the Minnesota checkpoint, so I stopped at a truck stop in Sauk Centre. When I entered the service station to use the rest room, I asked the clerk if she knew what kind of weather I could expect to encounter ahead.

"An eastbound driver just told me he was hit pretty hard coming through," she replied. "He said he was having trouble keeping his rig straight in the high winds."

I don't often stop for heavy rain, as long as I'm wearing the proper gear, so we continued west. Jeff took the lead, followed by Scott. I brought up the rear. After only a few miles, we encountered heavy rain and very strong winds. It was obvious from the heavy spray the motorcycle was generating and from the resistance of the front tire against the water that it was collecting on the road faster than could be drained away.

"Well, what do you want to do now?" Scott's voice cracked over the CB. "Do you want to try to bust through?"

I considered Scott's question for a few moments before replying. It was nearly 3:00 a.m. and I hadn't slept for almost 20 hours. My next scheduled rest stop was 18 hours and 1,100 miles away in Sidney, Nebraska. I knew I couldn't make it to Sidney, via the Dakotas, Montana, and Wyoming, without sleep. I decided it would be better to nap while a raging storm passed, rather than ride through such severe conditions. We were only a short distance from the last fuel stop. If we continued, we might not be able to find a convenient place to stop later.

I had no idea how far Jeff was ahead of us, and his motorcycle wasn't equipped with a CB. I hoped he would decide to turn around too.

My left thumb reached for the "talk" button.

"I'm for turning back to the last fuel stop and grabbing a nap until this thing blows over," I replied. "I'd rather not deal with this crap right now."

"I understand," Scott replied. "Let's do a U-turn at the next crossover."

By now the wind was so violent that the motorcycle was being shoved several feet from side-to-side. The visibility was so low that we had difficulty recognizing the crossovers, even riding well below the speed limit.

I recognized a crossover just as Scott's motorcycle passed it. It came up so quickly that neither of us could have safely turned into it.

"You just passed one, Scott," I spoke into the microphone.

"I know. I didn't see it in time," Scott answered as his left turn signal flashed and he drifted his motorcycle to the right shoulder. "Let's go back and get it."

The highway was deserted, so we executed a U-turn and rode east in the westbound lane until we reached the crossover.

The clerk was waiting at the door when we returned to the truck stop.

"Decided to sit it out for a while, huh?" she smiled. "You guys make yourselves at home and I'll put on a fresh pot of coffee. I'd be happy to warm up a nice sweet roll for you too, if you'd like."

"Thanks anyway," I replied. "I don't care for anything. Is there a driver's lounge with a couch where I can grab a quick nap?"

"There's no couch, but we have a driver's lounge where you can sit if you'd like. How about your motorcycles? Would you like to park them in the shed behind the station?"

"That would be great," I replied. There wasn't any cover available for the motorcycles in front of the station and I welcomed the opportunity to get the bikes protected without having to take time to get out the rain cover.

"We had another rider with us, so if he comes back, would you please let him know we've parked the bikes back there?" I asked.

After placing our motorcycles in the storage shed, Scott and I returned to the driver's lounge, where I prepared to take a nap while sitting in a chair.

"How long do you want to nap?" Scott asked. "Do you want me to wake you at a specific time?"

"Let's say an hour or so. I'd like to give it enough time to let the storm pass."

I knew I wouldn't be able to nap for very long while sitting in the chair. But I also knew I'd have no trouble getting to sleep. I relished the opportunity to close my eyes while the storm worked its way by.

I didn't know it at the time, but as I sat in the chair and leaned my head against the wall that separated the driver's lounge from one of the shower rooms for the truckers, Scott was

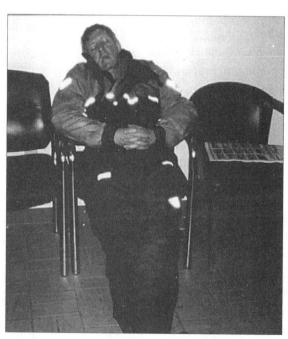

Ron sleeps in a truck stop during the thunderstorm in Minnesota, just after 2 a.m. (photo by Scott Ward).

listening to a lot of laughter and some other interesting sounds coming from the other side of the wall.

"After nearly an hour, a trucker emerged from the shower area with a poker face, but the woman who followed him out the door blushed red right down to her toes," Scott later reported. "She only looked me in the eye for a second or two and then looked away and turned bright red as they headed for the door. I enjoyed the opportunity to give both of them a knowing smile as they left the lounge."

Less than an hour and a half had passed when I awoke. Scott was standing in the driver's lounge, considering waking me. I suggested that we walk outside to see if the storm had passed. The sky to the west was clear. The air had a fresh smell that is so characteristic after a rain. We retrieved our bikes from the shed and continued to Fargo.

35 - North Dakota
Adam Wolkoff arrived in Fargo early, after riding through the storm. The Mobil station was closed, but the automatic "pay at the pump" was available.

North Dakota checkpoint: Scott Ward, Gary "Oly"Olson, Ron, and Adam Wolkoff. Gary lost his job because he got so swept up in accompanying Ron.

Back at home, Barbara was startled awake by the sound of the phone ringing. Glancing at the clock, she saw that it was 3:20 a.m. and immediately assumed the worst.

"Hi. Have you heard anything since Wisconsin?" Adam asked.

Since it was only five minutes past my scheduled arrival in Fargo, Barbara wasn't concerned and quickly fell back to sleep.

At 5:00 a.m., Adam called again. This time I was late and Barbara began to worry. Adam professed to feeling bad about calling her so early, but was eager to learn if there had been any changes in the schedule. As there had been no news since Wisconsin, Adam went back to waiting.

"As I sat at the empty gas station, no fewer than eight squad cars cruised by," Adam reported. "I kept wanting one to stop, for the entertainment value such an encounter would have provided, but no luck."

"Several hours later, Jeff Lambert showed up," Adam wrote in a report to LDRIDER.

He hadn't seen Ron in some time. As we swapped '97 Iron Butt stories, a local rider pulled in, and introduced himself as 'Oly.' When we told him about Ron's attempt, he became visibly excited. After waiting a while, he reluctantly left for work and Jeff and I resumed our conversation.

A short while later Oly returned. He was so taken with Ron's quest that he decided to bag work for the day in favor of witness duty.

Around 6:30 a.m., Scott Ward pulled in, with Ron close behind. Ron and Scott had chosen to wait out the storm Jeff and I had ridden through.

Ron was his usual friendly self, and was much more alert and talkative than I would have expected, after what he has been going through.

After we all signed the witness log, we sat around chatting. Photos were taken, and Ron consumed another of the now ubiquitous bananas.

While trying to recruit witnesses for some of my hardship posts, I had held Adam's name in reserve. Adam offered to meet me at Inver Grove Heights, which was close to his home. I didn't expect difficulty recruiting Minnesota witnesses, so I told Adam that I planned to impose on him for a more interesting location.

"Thanks for volunteering for Minnesota," I wrote. "I hope it doesn't sound too presumptuous, but I was planning to call you when things got tough and I needed someone to meet me in some godforsaken place at 3:00 a.m."

Adam's response was exactly what I expected.

"Cool. You call, I'll go."

The godforsaken place would be Fargo. By Iron Butt standards, the 240-mile distance wasn't so bad, but the 3:15 a.m. estimated arrival time was cruel. That's probably why he decided to have Barbara join the party.

After Adam introduced me to Oly, I gave him one of my circulars with the route map and my schedule. Oly was pleased that I welcomed having him join Scott and me as we headed for Montana. As the paper signing was being performed I peeled

Ron, Scott Ward, and Gary Olson prepare to leave a gas stop in western North Dakota (photo by Scott Ward).

another banana. "If you get to the point of needing additional motivation, you should dangle a banana on a string in front of your helmet," Adam suggested wryly.

Jeff considered continuing with us, but he had already ridden more than he'd intended and decided to head home to Rapids City, Illinois. He had traveled about 700 miles since leaving home and would reach a total of about 1,300 for the trip by the time he got back. I thanked him for his help in escorting me through the unfamiliar roads in Illinois and Wisconsin.

Although I now had only 14 more states to visit, I knew that North Dakota marked only the halfway point in the distance my trip entailed. And I was three hours behind schedule.

Day	State	Miles Ridden	Miles to Go
4	35	4,341	4,457

36 - Montana

Shortly after leaving Fargo, Oly pulled his motorcycle beside mine and motioned to his fuel tank, then his watch, then held up three fingers. He repeated the sequence of signals several times. I returned the OK sign, acknowledging that he needed three minutes to stop and refuel. In the excitement of preparing to join the journey, he hadn't thought about filling up in Fargo.

When Oly asked to ride with me I told him I wouldn't stop until I needed fuel. I waved to him as he turned for the exit ramp, then pressed the talk switch on the CB.

"That will probably be the last we see of Oly," I remarked to Scott, regretfully. We were traveling at a very spirited pace and I didn't expect him to make up for the time he would lose with a fuel stop.

Within a few minutes, my radar detector fired and we slowed as we passed a state trooper who was partially hidden under a highway overpass.

"If Oly does try to catch us, he'll never make it past that Smoky," Scott remarked. "I don't think he was running a radar detector."

A half hour later, Oly pulled beside me on his red BMW and displayed an enthusiastic "thumbs up" signal. I could see his wide grin inside his helmet. When we stopped for fuel in Tappen, Oly acknowledged that he expected to be ticketed when he flew past the parked trooper.

"I was running wide open when I passed him," Oly admitted. "He must have either been sleeping, or he realized there was no way he could catch me at the speed I was traveling."

As we passed Exit 42 where I-94 intersects Route 85, I recalled how, in the summer of 1996, I participated in the Miles Incorporated Rally sponsored by Reno BMW. The rally was 36 hours in duration and started and ended in Ely, Nevada. Each rider selected his own route, and the objective of the rally was to ride as many miles as possible in 36 hours. At the rider dinner the night before the rally, riders were asked to comment on the route they had selected.

"I'm planning to ride from here to Rugby, North Dakota, and back," I announced. "Rugby is the geographical center of North America. I thought it would be appropriate to use it as the turnaround point for this ride."

I ran out of time before reaching Rugby, and instead headed south on Route 85 at Williston, North Dakota, then got on I-94 here at Exit 42. I finished the rally in third place after riding 2,639 miles. Steve Losofsky won after riding more than 3,027 miles and his business partner, Jan Cutler, finished second with 2,893 miles.

As Oly, Scott, and I traveled across North Dakota, DeVern Gerber, Bill Weyher, and George Barnes were having breakfast in Glendive, Montana. DeVern and Bill had arrived the night before, taking a motel room across the street from the Conoco station I had selected as the Montana checkpoint. The shortest route I could devise for Montana, Wyoming, and South Dakota called for stops in Alzada, Montana, and Colony, Wyoming; towns with fewer than 30 residents each. When I couldn't locate a business establishment in either location, I selected Glendive, Montana, and Sundance, Wyoming instead.

DeVern and Bill traveled more than 750 miles from their homes in Utah. George rode almost 900 miles from Carbondale, Colorado, riding straight through for eleven hours. All three had participated in the Iron Butt Rally in 1997 in addition to

the Utah 1088 and other endurance events. George won the
Utah 1088 in 1996 and Bill won it the following year.

During their breakfast, Bill called Barbara and learned
that I was running late. The trio pulled out their maps and
worked on developing a route for Montana, South Dakota, and
Wyoming that would shave time and distance from my plan.

They made a quick trip to a service station at Wibaux,
Montana, the first town I would encounter after crossing the
state line from North Dakota. Once assured that the station
could provide a valid receipt, the group waited on the shoulder
of the interstate to intercept me as I entered Montana.

While I handled the signatures and photograph in Wibaux,
George described the new plan. We would go south on Route 7 to
Baker, Montana, then east to Bowman, North Dakota, and
south to Buffalo, where we would perform the witness ceremo-
nies for South Dakota.

Day	State	Miles Ridden	Miles to Go
4	36	4,701	4,097

Montana checkpoint: Ron, George Barnes, Bill Weyher, and DeVern
Gerber.

DeVern Gerber led the way and I rode in the middle of the pack. We slowed as we entered the small Montana town of Baker. My radar unit fired and I saw a state trooper traveling in our direction. I tapped the brakes and reached for the talk button to warn those behind me. As I checked my rearview mirror, I saw the trooper's strobe lights begin to flash as the patrol car executed a U-turn. A moment later, Scott delivered the bad news.

"I'm afraid it's too late, Ron. He's pulling us over."

The trooper pulled Scott and George over and we remaining four continued toward Bowman, North Dakota, then to Buffalo, South Dakota. Scott and George had intended to continue with us, but we didn't see them again after Baker. Although I hadn't requested, or even suggested, that any friends or volunteers subject themselves to the risk of a traffic violation to help me, several riders volunteered to lead the way, specifically to take the "hit" for me if we encountered radar. Ironically, the only tickets issued occurred while riders were following me.

Months after my ride, I would learn the outcome of Scott's attempt at endurance certification. Scott later wrote:

Riding with you from Minnesota through Montana and then meeting up again in Nebraska is a portion of time, thought, riding, adventure, and life experience I will cherish and smile about for many years. It was one of a chosen few motorcycling high points of 1998.

I have told the story more than once about those friends of yours waiting for us at the overpass just inside the Montana border with a new route and our quick trip toward the South Dakota border. Too bad I ended up donating to the state's highway department and missed the next part of that ride. The excitement that group had, and the positive energy they all generated for your record-setting trip was a huge shot in the arm. It confirmed to me that the long-distance riding community was real, and had its share of top-quality members.

That quick trip was also invigorating! That section of the trip inspired me to go harder, ride longer, and

South Dakota checkpoint: DeVern Gerber, Ron, and Bill Weyher.

Wyoming checkpoint: Ron, Bill Weyher, and Ren Berggren.

*really test and at the same time build myself. It was so
much more than a drive on a motorcycle.*

*I did complete 1,500 miles in 36 hours on that trip.
Then the national parks in Utah, and a quick
SaddleSore 1000 ride home.*

37 - South Dakota
We continued to Belle Fourche where we picked up I-90 for
Sundance, Wyoming. Just before Belle Fourche, a trooper
stopped DeVern and delayed him for a long conversation.

"After the usual check of my paperwork, the conversation
turned to the weather, progressed to the joys of traveling by motorcycle, law enforcement as a career, whether or not I liked my
BMW, the additional fuel cell on the back of the motorcycle, and
so on. The conversation finally ended with a warning."

Day	State	Miles Ridden	Miles to Go
4	37	4,835	3,963

38 - Wyoming
Ren Berggren from Longmont, Colorado, was waiting when
Bill, Oly, and I pulled into the Conoco station in Sundance. After the witnessing ritual was complete and I began setting up to
take a photograph, DeVern pulled into the station and told us
about his delay.

I called Barbara to give her an update. After fond farewells
and thanks to Bill and DeVern for their escort, Oly and I headed
for Nebraska via Cheyenne.

Day	State	Miles Ridden	Miles to Go
4	38	4,947	3,851

39 - Nebraska
It was almost 9:00 p.m. when we arrived at the Days Inn in Sidney for a much-needed rest. I was almost two hours late. Although Oly was more than 700 miles from his home in Fargo, he
had traveled through five states, riding almost 1,000 miles in
the last 15 hours. He wished me well for the rest of the ride,
thanked me once again for inviting him to join me, and headed

Nebraska checkpoint: Tony Black, Norm Babcock, Ron, Linda
Babcock, and Tom Vervaeke.

for home. I would later learn of an unfortunate consequence of
Oly's spontaneous enthusiasm and participation in my ride.

Tony Black, Tom Vervaeke, and Norm and Linda Babcock
were waiting for me at the motel in Sidney. Norm and Linda
were riding matching BMW F650 motorcycles, each with a set
of "knobby" off-road tires strapped on top of their luggage racks.
Norm has not only participated in numerous Alberta 2000s as
well as the 8/48, he once set a world's record by driving a Volvo
PV-444 sports car a distance of 9,261 miles, hitting the 48 contiguous states, Canada, and Mexico in 8 days, 4 hours, and 13
minutes.

The Babcocks were planning to meet me in Hyder, Alaska,
to help celebrate the end of the 49-state ride. Then they planned
to travel extensively in Alaska for several weeks. Their route to
Hyder from Sidney would require riding more than 2,000 miles.
I would ride almost 3,500 miles through nine more states to get
there. Less than 64 hours remained if I was going to finish the
49-state ride in less than a week.

Tony's son Jeff had volunteered for another of my tough locations: Limon, Colorado, at 2:30 a.m. Jeff would then escort me to Colorado Springs where I would pick up I-25 for my trip to Santa Fe. I had scheduled a four-hour stop in Sidney, but I now planned to cut it by at least 30 minutes to insure I would make it to Limon on time. Tony agreed to call Jeff with my estimated arrival time for Limon.

As I was preparing for my third motel stop since leaving Kittery almost 100 hours ago, Pat Widder notified LDRIDER about his planned participation in the event. Pat, owner of Widder Enterprises in Ojai, California, the leading manufacturer of heated clothing for motorcyclists, had arranged to set up his "Widder-CAM," to transmit live images to the Internet from the California checkpoint:

Tomorrow (6/12) we will hopefully be sending live shots of Ron from Needles, California. I say hopefully, because if I can't "persuade" the Texaco guys to let us use a land line, it will be by cellular connection. "If" the signal is good enough, the uploads will be painfully slow, as it will only connect at 14.4 baud.

You'll also be able to chat with anyone else at the page if you wish. If for some reason the chat thing doesn't work for you, I'm afraid I won't be able to help.

Rob Lentini or Jeff Powell will be calling us from the Arizona checkpoint when Ron departs, so hopefully we'll have a good idea of his ETA.

Unless Ron is running way late or way early, we'll start broadcasting at about 4:15 p.m. PDT.

Day	State	Miles Ridden	Miles to Go
5	39	5,316	3,482

United States

400 km

0   400 Miles

Wendover

Ely

NV

UT

Sidney

CO   Limon

CA

Needles Kingman AZ   NM

Santa Fe

8

Nebraska to Utah

The weather was great when I left the motel and headed for Limon, Colorado, but I was a little apprehensive about riding alone. The route seemed straightforward, but from prior experience, I knew that a wrong turn at this time of the morning in unfamiliar terrain could cost a lot of time. When I arrived in Attwood at 1:10 a.m., I checked the map, then asked a service station attendant to confirm I was heading for Limon.

40 - Colorado

In addition to Jeff Black, Brad Hogue, who had also been at the Iowa checkpoint, Tim Moffitt and Brian Boberick were also at the Limon stop.

After refueling, the group provided fresh bananas and cold water for the jug. I signed Brian's copy of *Against the Wind,* and followed Jeff to Colorado Springs. We were in Jeff's "stomping grounds" and he guided me through backroad shortcuts for the 70 miles to I-25 near Colorado Springs.

Day	State	Miles Ridden	Miles to Go
5	40	5,467	3,331

We exchanged waves shortly before 4:00 a.m. when Jeff took the exit for home.

Before I reached Colorado City, I became so sleepy that I pulled into a rest area, set the Screaming Meanie for 60 minutes and lay down on a nearby picnic table. The surface of the

Colorado checkpoint: Tim Moffitt, Chris Lawson, Ron, Brian
Boberick, and Brad Hogue.

table, a metal grate material, was different from any other I
had encountered at a rest area, but when I lay on it, I couldn't
tell the difference between it and concrete tables I had become
familiar with at Iron Butt Motels—or from my mattress at
home. The Iron Butt Motel is a term that has been used to describe sleeping on (or very near) the motorcycle. For me, this
usually means a bench or picnic table at a rest area. I sometimes sleep on the motorcycle if a bench or table isn't available.

Less than ten miles after leaving the rest area, I stopped in
Colorado City for fuel, then stopped again in Springer, New
Mexico. It was nearly 8:00 a.m. when I exited the filling station
in Springer. Ira Agins had been at the Giant service station in
Santa Fe for a half-hour, in anticipation of my arriving at 8:30
a.m. I looked at my route sheet and estimated that my arrival in
Santa Fe would be about an hour behind schedule.

Barbara would be leaving Dallas later in the afternoon to
fly to Vancouver, where she would stay overnight. In the morn-

ing she would fly to Terrace, British Columbia, rent a car, and drive several hours to Hyder to await my arrival.

As I was heading for the New Mexico checkpoint, Barbara was posting an announcement that would cause quite a stir.

BULLETIN FROM THE CONTROL CENTER: *I (Barbara) will be leaving late this afternoon to begin my trip to Hyder, Alaska, to greet Ron. So the New Mexico checkpoint is the last update I will be able to make to this web site. Ron said that as soon as he gets to Alaska (and maybe after he gets some sleep) he will post an update. The 800 number will continue to be covered by my sister, Roberta, to help coordinate the checkpoints.*

Those following my progress were incredulous to think that now, as I was beginning the fourth leg of my journey, updates would stop until I was done. When Barbara and I had discussed this plan, we had envisioned the web site merely as a tool for co-ordinating witnesses. We hadn't realized the role it would play in keeping those who were not LDRIDER subscribers informed. At this point, the web site had received more than 2,000 "hits" since my ride began five days earlier.

In reflecting on the interest with which riders were following my progress, Howard Chain later wrote:

The interest and hunger for information built slowly at first, but after you were at least a third to half the way through, the LDRIDER "media frenzy" was on. When it looked like you were going to make it, everyone was going nuts for updates, and toward the end, when your wife left the nerve center to go to Alaska—oh boy!

Norm Grills and Dale Wilson both offered to perform the updates, but Barbara didn't know how to describe the passwords and protocols for gaining access to the web pages. To make it easy for her, I had automated most of the process and taught her only enough to do simple updates to preformatted pages.

After numerous appeals not to interrupt the updates, Barbara recruited my 22-year-old son Brad to the task. The

electronic audience welcomed Barbara's revised announcement:

> MODIFICATION TO ABOVE BULLETIN: *Due to
> popular request I have made arrangements to have
> this web page continue to be updated after I leave.
> Ron's son, Brad, will be posting checkpoint arrivals
> and other pertinent information that we receive.*

Brad came to the house on his lunch breaks and again immediately after work to perform the updates.

41 - New Mexico

As I approached Exit 282, my designated turnoff for the Giant
station checkpoint in Santa Fe, I saw Dave Beck on the shoulder on his Buell, waiting to escort me to the service station. We
exchanged waves as I passed, then he quickly caught up and
signaled for me to follow.

As we pulled into the station, I recognized Ira Agins, waiting with about a dozen other riders, including witnesses Jeffery

New Mexico checkpoint: Ron and Ira Agins (in hat), (others
unidentified).

Foster and Jim Hickerson. Jerry Harris, Stan Fisher, and Lyle Williams had also turned out.

In addition to the bananas Ira provided, he had prepared a detailed weather briefing for my ride to Arizona, including a color printout from an Internet weather page. While Ira and I talked, others checked the tire pressure and cleaned the bugs and dirt from my windshield and lights.

"You won't have any rain to deal with," Ira stated, "but you'll have some strong winds pretty soon. The good thing is, they should be tailwinds."

Like Scott Ward, Jeffery Foster also wanted to perform an Iron Butt certification ride within my 7/49 ride. Jeff had attempted a Bun Burner Gold ride the previous October, but fell short of his goal, taking 27 hours to complete the 1,500-mile ride. Jeff admitted he hadn't been properly prepared for the cold weather he'd encountered, and he'd tarried too long warming up at rest stops. Jeff had established two riding goals for 1998. The first was to complete a Bun Burner Gold ride, and the second was to complete the IBA National Parks Tour, which required visiting 50 or more National Parks in at least 25 different states in one year. A "passport" would have to be stamped at the visitor center in each park.

When Jeff learned of my ride, he agreed to meet me in New Mexico. He then planned to ride to Washington, pick up some National Park passport stamps along the way, and would finish his 1,500 miles before reaching Clarkston, Washington. From there, he would head to my Kennewick checkpoint and secure my signature on his witness form, thereby obtaining my signature at both the beginning and end of his ride.

After signing a copy of *Against the Wind* for one of the riders, I thanked Ira for the weather briefing and headed to Albuquerque with Jerry Harris and Stan Fisher in tow.

Day	State	Miles Ridden	Miles to Go
5	41	5,860	2,938

I hoped that when I reached I-40 at Albuquerque, I'd be able to make up for the hour I was behind. About 15 miles north of Albuquerque, traffic came to a stop at a construction zone. There was only one lane open and traffic was stop and go, as several lanes merged into one. Stan pulled beside me, flipped his face shield open, and shouted, "Sorry about this."

Stan had been aware of the construction work and potential delay before we left Santa Fe, and he even knew a useful detour around the area. But several people who recently traveled that portion of I-25 assured him that we wouldn't have any problems. Of course, we encountered the delay immediately after passing the last exit that would have allowed the detour around the construction. Stan felt responsible for our becoming ensnarled in the traffic jam. If I had known about his efforts, I would have assured him it wasn't his fault.

After the merge was complete, we were riding at no more than 20 mph for several miles. Finally, we cleared the construction zone and were able to travel at faster speeds. Jerry Harris wanted to accompany me to Flagstaff, but instead turned off at the Paso del Norte Exit a few miles north of I-40, submitting to the pressure of new job commitments.

Leaving Albuquerque, I followed I-40 to Grants. There aren't many parts of the United States that don't evoke memories of some endurance event. It was here that one of my Oklahoma witnesses, Ardys Kellerman, had an accident during the 1995 Iron Butt Rally and was unable to finish. She and I had met a little further west, at the Meteor Crater bonus location, just hours before her accident.

I continued through the San Mateo and Zuni Mountains, encountering strong cross winds. These became very aggravating, as I frequently found myself fighting to keep the motorcycle positioned properly in my lane. I looked forward to reaching Needles, California, where I expected my northerly ride to be accompanied by strong tail winds.

42 - Arizona

I descended to the Colorado Plateau and stopped for fuel again in Holbrook, the official Host City for the Petrified Forest and Painted Desert.

I continued toward Flagstaff, looking forward to the 2,000-foot climb that I expected would provide cooler temperatures. On several previous occasions, snow and ice have prevented my taking I-40 from the West Coast back to Texas. At such times, I've taken the longer route on I-10 through Phoenix and El Paso. On this ride, however, I welcomed the cooler temperatures.

Although I'd never seen elk in the area, I began to see a lot of signs warning of them. As I passed the rest area on my left, I remembered that I'd often looked forward to that stop for a quick nap.

In this part of the country, I-40 has replaced old Route 66. I've always been interested in this historic route and have read a lot about it. My route from Santa Fe to Needles, California, followed the old Route 66. In 1987, the Historic Route 66 Association of Arizona was formed. Similar groups have formed in many other cities along the old highway to promote its historic significance. Much of the highway follows centuries-old Indian trails. Through the years, Route 66 has had many names: The Main Street of America, the Wire Road, Will Rogers Highway, and the Mother Road, to name a few. Route 66 is probably the most well-known highway in the United States, if not the world, and it seems to hold a different meaning for everyone who takes the time to see it.

When I was in my early twenties, a friend and I drove my small Triumph Spitfire, a sports car weighing little more than some of today's large touring motorcycles, from Baltimore, through Mexico, to the Guatemalan border and back. We were inspired, at least in part, by a TV program at the time called "Route 66." The program was about two young men who traveled the country in a Corvette. One of my favorite mementos of the trip is a photograph of me posing with my car beneath a Route 66 sign in Missouri. Little did I know I'd still be wandering this old road thirty years later.

While reading about the history of this famous highway, I learned how Flagstaff was named. On the 4th of July in 1876, as the United States turned 100, a group of people built a flagpole out of a pine tree to raise the American flag in Antelope

Ron arrives in Kingman, Arizona (photo by Dennis Robinson).

Rob Lentini signs the witness form for Ron's ride (photo by Dennis Robinson).

Ron recuperates in Arizona (photo by Dennis Robinson).

Arizona checkpoint: Denny Robinson, Jeff Powell, Ron, Rob Lentini, and Pablo Garcia.

Park. Seven years later, the Atlantic and Pacific Railroad (later
to become the Santa Fe) was constructed through Antelope
Park. The city was then named for the flagstaff, which was still
standing.

The temperature began to rise again as I began my descent
from the San Francisco Mountains to the Coconino Plateau.
During my 150-mile ride to Kingman, I would drop 3,500 feet in
altitude. Pablo Garcia, Rob Lentini, Dennis Robinson and his
wife Roberta, and Jeff Powell were awaiting my arrival there.
Rob, a director of the BMW Owners Association, and Pablo Garcia had ridden 320 miles from their homes in Tucson. The
Robinsons had ridden about 100 miles less coming from Chan-
dler. Jeff, a resident of Kingman, was in his own neighborhood.
During the stop, Dennis and Roberta took photographs, several
of which turned out to be some of my favorites from the ride.

Before I announced plans for the 7/49, Pablo Garcia sent me
an e-mail complimenting me on *Against the Wind.* He was interested in pursuing endurance riding because of the amount of
riding that he could accomplish in a limited time:

*This will allow me to put a lot of effort into something
I really love into a limited schedule. In other words,
I'm quite sure I can get a 'kitchen pass' for a few days.
I once suggested to my wife that I wanted to take about
a year off and break the world record for the number of
countries visited by motorcycle. She promised that she
would be nowhere in sight when I got back. So as you
can see, endurance riding can work for me.*

Day	State	Miles Ridden	Miles to Go
5	42	6,387	2,411

I have always enjoyed the scenery between Kingman and
Needles. Although I-40 is a major east/west highway, it turns
abruptly to the south at Kingman, continues south for about 40
miles, turns to the west for fifteen miles or so, then turns back
to the north as the highway heads to Needles, California. From
Kingman to Needles, I-40 circles the Warm Springs Wilderness,
an immense and pristine desert. One thousand feet above the
surrounding desert, the ten-mile-long Black Mesa dominates

the landscape. Its edges are dissected into a maze of winding canyons, and the surrounding plain is dotted with remnant mesas and isolated hills.

43- California

Witnesses Pat Widder, Jim White, and Scott Lee rode nearly 250 miles from the Los Angeles area to Needles. Pat had been following my progress and assumed that I would arrive late in California, as I had been running late for the last few days. Instead, I had been making great time from Kingman and arrived in California on schedule. As I pulled into the service station, I seemed to take the group by surprise.

"I think the thing that impressed me most was how cool, calm, and collected you were," Pat later told me. "Jim, Scott, and I had been standing around kickin' tires for about an hour before you touched down in Needles. We received a call from the Arizona checkpoint saying you had left there 30 minutes ago. A quick calculation concluded you would be arriving very soon. We had just got the computer online for the live feed when you arrived. Then it seemed like we were three monkeys running

California checkpoint: Jim White, Scott Lee, Ron, and Pat Widder.

Pat Widder
poses with his
bike (photo by
Pat Widder).

around trying to play pit crew while you calmly munched on a
banana and orchestrated the whole procedure for us for the
43rd time. Impressed the hell outa me!"

After refueling, I handed my camera to the gas station attendant and asked him to take a picture of us. I had placed a
Widder "Lectric-Heat" sticker on my windshield, and another
on the rear of the motorcycle, under the license plate. When we
first posed for the picture, Pat was blocking the view of the
sticker on the windshield, so I suggested that he move aside for
another shot. I've always appreciated Pat's support of endurance riding events and wanted to be sure that my pride in using
his products was evident in the photograph.

Day	State	Miles Ridden	Miles to Go
6	43	6,447	2,351

44 - Nevada
When I planned the ride, I didn't try to plan fuel stops, except
for checkpoint locations. In fact, checkpoint stops would take

care of most refueling requirements, but I naively expected fuel to be readily available in between the checkpoints.

Even before reaching Exit 64 of I-15 for Route 93 beyond North Las Vegas, I had started to look for an opportunity to buy gas. When I reached the exit, I noted that I had traveled 134 miles since refueling. I had equipped my motorcycle with a novel computerized unit: Fuel Plus. The unit was integrated with the fuel injection system and provided very accurate readings of range, average speed, and many other statistics that I found useful. It was now indicating an available range of about 50 miles. I didn't know that my next opportunity to buy fuel was 75 miles away. As I continued, I realized that I might be creating a worse situation by getting to the point where I couldn't even backtrack to a gasoline station on my remaining fuel.

I finally stopped to consult a map. I hadn't seen signs for Alamo yet. Although I wasn't certain exactly where I was, I was sure I'd run out of gas before I arrived there.

I continued, but dropped my speed to about 40 mph. There was very little traffic on the road and it was often more than five minutes between the times I would see another vehicle. My Fuel Plus unit indicated a range of less than 20 miles when I saw my first signpost to Alamo—45 miles away.

A short distance to the west of the highway, an 18-wheeler was preparing to exit a gravel pit. I decided it would be smarter to try to obtain gas where there was some sign of civilization, rather than to continue riding until I was stranded. It began to rain as I turned on to the unpaved strip of road leading toward the gravel pit.

I approached the driver of the semi as he was checking the pressure in his tires.

"I'm about to run out of gasoline. Can you tell me how far I'd have to ride, in either direction, to find fuel?"

"Well, it's probably 50 miles back to the closest gas on the interstate, if you're heading to Las Vegas," he answered.

"I'm riding north, to Ely. How far before I find some gas in that direction?"

"I can't say for sure. I've never been in that direction. I just run back and forth between here and Las Vegas."

"How ironic that this professional driver's travels have been so limiting," I thought.

The driver seemed friendly and appeared to be the type of chap who would help if he could. For a moment, I considered asking him for a ride back to the nearest gasoline station, thinking I might be able to find a ride back to get the motorcycle. Then I thought about the can of worms I might be opening by leaving the motorcycle unattended, here in the desert.

"I don't suppose you have any gasoline with you," I asked, knowing that his truck used diesel. "Or, is there anyone else out here at this operation that might have some?"

"No, I don't have any. You might check with some of the workers down at the pit," the driver responded, pointing to the west, toward a gravel pit. I hadn't realized there were automobiles in the area, as they were hidden from view by scrub brush and low sand dunes.

I thanked the driver and continued down the dirt road for another half mile. As I approached a small group of metal sheds, I had to weave my way around high piles of gravel in the middle of a large lot. I came upon a gravel loader that was adding to the height of one of the piles. Although the ground wasn't slippery yet, I thought about how slick the area would get if the rain continued. Two cars and a pickup truck were parked a short distance away.

I parked the motorcycle, removed my helmet and earplugs, and walked toward the loader, waving to the operator to attract his attention. He acknowledged my wave, turned off the engine, and climbed down into the muddy lot. Although he didn't look like he'd reached his 40th birthday yet, he appeared to have a lot of miles on his body. He was about six feet tall and probably weighed close to 300 pounds. Most of his weight was concentrated from his belt to an area about five or six inches above it. He was wearing filthy, faded blue jeans, a dirty, torn T-shirt, heavy work boots, and a hard hat. The term "Bubba" came immediately to mind.

"Well, I suppose I know who the pickup belongs to," I thought. "If this were Texas, there would be a rifle rack in the rear window and a cooler chest on the front seat."

"I'm about out of gas," I said. "I know I can't make it to Alamo from here. Any chance I can buy some from you or someone else here?"

"Well, all this stuff runs on *diesel*," Bubba answered in a slow drawl. "I think we have some gas around here *someplace* though. Let's go have a *look*," he said as he headed for a group of dilapidated, rusting metal equipment sheds. I was amused at how Bubba emphasized at least one word in each sentence that he spoke. I felt a pang of guilt for being critical of someone who seemed so willing to help me out of my self-induced predicament.

"Diesel," Bubba mumbled as he opened a drum and sniffed the contents. He went from one battered storage can to another, repeating the process of removing the cap, sniffing the contents and replacing the cap. He led the way into another shed, glancing around for gasoline. I stayed on his heels like a hungry puppy hoping for a meal.

Convinced there wasn't any fuel available, Bubba started across the lot toward a trailer that served as an office for the operation.

"Let's go ask the *super*," Bubba muttered as we walked in the direction of the trailer.

"This man needs *gas*," Bubba announced as he entered the trailer with me following behind. "I checked the *sheds*, but the only thing we got out *there* is *diesel*."

Bubba leaned back against the wall of the trailer and crossed his arms. He seemed pleased to present the supervisor with my dilemma. Now he wanted to observe how the situation turned out. I think he was motivated as much from having an excuse to stop working for awhile, as he was from interest in helping me.

"Yeah, I think we cleaned out all the gas last week and sent it into town," the supervisor replied. "I'll radio Ed and see if he left any behind."

The supervisor picked up his hand-held radio and called to Ed.

"Ed, stop down here at the office will you?" the supervisor asked.

"Will do," came the crackled reply.

I wondered why the supervisor didn't simply ask Ed if he knew where to find gasoline, rather than ask him to take the time to come to the office. I was pleased that both Bubba and the supervisor appeared to be willing to invest some effort to help.

I glanced at my watch, apprehensive about the time I was wasting. I wondered if there wasn't a way to do something productive. I was tired, but this didn't seem like an appropriate time to take a nap.

As I waited for Ed to arrive, a semi pulled into the lot and Bubba ambled to the door. "Well, back to *work*," Bubba mumbled as he headed for his loader. I watched as he extended his hand to reach a handle on the side of the loader, pulled himself up into the cab, started the engine, and began transferring gravel from one of the piles into the waiting truck.

Before Bubba finished loading the truck, another loader pulled into the lot. A slightly built man of about thirty descended from the machine and walked into the office. "What's up?" Ed asked, as he entered the office.

"This motorcycle rider here needs some gas," the supervisor replied. "Have we got any around here, or did we clean the whole place out of it last week?"

"I sent it all to the other site," Ed responded. "Didn't think we had any use for it around here," he continued. "All our stuff runs on diesel."

Bubba returned from the loader, lunch pail in hand, and leaned against a table that had been fashioned by attaching a 4 x 8 sheet of plywood to one wall of the trailer. "*Lunch* time," Bubba announced as he extracted a sandwich from the lunch pail.

"Well, how about letting me siphon a few gallons from one of your cars," I asked. I'd be happy to make it worth your while."

The absence of a response and the suspension of eye contact suggested this wasn't an idea they welcomed. It was several seconds before Bubba responded.

"I live a long *way* from here. I only have enough gas to get *home*."

"Can't you sell me enough to get to Alamo and still have enough to get there to buy more for yourself?" I asked.

"But I'm not *going* to Alamo," Bubba responded. "I live the other *way*." He seemed to enjoy having an excuse to keep me in my predicament.

"How much gas do you need?" Ed asked softly.

"Just enough to get to Alamo," I replied. "As little as a gallon would probably do it."

"Well, I guess I could sell you a gallon. I'll have to try to find something around here to siphon it with," he replied, as he headed out the office door for the storage sheds.

From the appearance of the sheds and the type of junk I saw when we looked through them a little earlier, I imagined that it wouldn't take long to find an old piece of hose. Worst case, I could offer to use the plastic drinking tube from my water reservoir, although I wasn't certain the tube was long enough. I decided to wait and see if Ed could find a piece of hose. I didn't want to unnecessarily contaminate my drinking tube.

After a few minutes of searching, Ed emerged with an old piece of hose that appeared long enough for the job. He picked up an old gallon tin can as he headed for the vehicles in the parking lot.

As Ed inserted the hose into his tank, I offered to perform the distasteful chore of providing the suction on the end of the hose.

"That's OK," Ed responded. "I'll get it going." Ed kneeled beside the car and began sucking on the end of the hose.

After several unsuccessful attempts, Ed removed the hose from the car's tank. The end of the hose was dry, indicating that the end hadn't reached the gas.

"Cars nowadays don't *let* you siphon," Bubba muttered as he sauntered up. "They have some kind of *contraption* that keeps people from *stealing* your gas."

I suspected he joined us as much to insure I wasn't trying to remove gasoline from his truck as to observe the process.

"Well, Ed, it looks like my options keep becoming fewer and fewer," I said. "Can I either hire you to drive me to Alamo to buy some gas, or rent your car from you for an hour or so?"

For the second time in the past ten minutes, I was greeted with silence. Ed obviously wasn't interested in loaning his car to a stranger who had ridden up on a motorcycle. It had been raining lightly since I pulled into the gravel pit, but now it began falling heavily.

"Let's get out of the rain while we figure out what to do," Ed remarked, as he and Bubba headed back for the trailer. I was still wearing rain gear and hadn't even noticed that I was the only one not getting wet.

As we entered the trailer, I decided to explore another option. "Where is the nearest place I can get road service?" I asked.

"The Chevron station in Alamo," the supervisor replied. "You want me to call them for you?"

"Yes, I'd appreciate it. Just let them know that I need to have them deliver a few gallons of gasoline here to the site."

The supervisor referred to a short list of phone numbers that were handwritten on a small piece of paper covered with very yellowed and brittle strips of cellophane tape.

"Alamo site here," the supervisor announced into the phone. "We've got a guy here on a motorcycle who's out of gas. Can you send a truck out?"

After a few moments pause, the supervisor turned to me. "Just a minute," he spoke into the receiver, then held it away from his mouth.

"Guy says it'll cost $145 plus the cost of the gas," he reported, as a sarcastic grin crept across his face.

"Great," I responded. "Just ask them how long before they can get here with it."

The supervisor's grin disappeared. He stared at me for several seconds, as if he didn't believe I was serious. He slowly raised the receiver to his mouth again. His demeanor reminded me of a blackjack dealer's reaction to a player who splits face cards, when the dealer is showing a five.

"The guy says OK. He wants to know how soon you can get here?"

"They say 45 minutes," the supervisor reported. Then, "Just a minute, I'll let you talk to him."

"They need a credit card number," he said, as he extended the receiver to me.

I opened my billfold and selected a credit card from the half-dozen that were clearly visible. I dictated the required information and placed the receiver back in its cradle. The trailer was quiet. Bubba resumed slowly chewing his sandwich. Ed stood against the wall with his arms crossed, looking nowhere in particular. The supervisor lit another cigarette and stared out the window at the gravel pit.

"You must need to get someplace real *bad* to pay 150 bucks for a can of *gas,*" Bubba finally remarked.

"Hey, I told you guys I'd be willing to make it worth your while to get me some gas," I chuckled. I expected this to lead to some creative thought from these guys, perhaps for the first time in their lives.

I started to enjoy my predicament. When I entered this gravel pit I needed something from these guys and was at the mercy of their generosity. Now my dilemma was solved. I had the upper hand. I no longer needed their help and had clearly achieved a position of dominance in our short acquaintance.

There hadn't been any reason to discuss the purpose of my trip, or where I was heading. I glanced at my watch. "Damn," I thought. "Just when I think I'm getting back on schedule, I blow it and get the timing all screwed up again."

Glancing at my watch intensified the perception that I was in a hurry.

"You got to get somewhere *quick* or something?" Bubba asked.

Thinking I'd probably wind up spending another hour here, I decided to discuss my ride and let the story unfold based on the level of interest exhibited by my hosts.

"I'm in the middle of an attempt to break the current record for visiting all 48 states on a motorcycle," I began. "I started in Maine last Sunday night and I've only got Utah, Idaho, Oregon, and Washington to go after this. I can't believe I was stupid enough to run out of gas, with all the planning I've put into this ride. You'd think I was an amateur."

The total lack of interest the workers had displayed in my motorcycle when I rode up indicated they weren't riders. The supervisor took a deep drag on his cigarette and looked off into the distance as he exhaled, as if to say, "Yeah right, and I'm the King of England."

"No kidding?" Ed responded. He looked as though he believed me, but offered no additional questions. It was as if there were some code between these guys that discouraged them from appearing easily impressed or gullible enough to buy some cock-and-bull story from a stranger. Ed seemed to be resisting an urge to ask for more information, however.

Bubba began paying much closer attention to me. He examined my riding suit with his eyes and appeared interested in knowing more. From his expression, I knew he was wondering about the cost of my riding suit and motorcycle. But Ed and Bubba probably felt that an expression of interest would be interpreted as a sign of weakness.

There was a long silence as the supervisor continued to smoke, Bubba began chewing on a long Tootsie Roll for desert, and Ed shuffled to the window to see how hard the rain was falling.

As Bubba finished his Tootsie Roll, crumpled the wrapper, and looked around the office for a trash can, he offered another question.

"You got *sponsors?*"

"Not enough to make a difference. This suit I'm wearing was offered to me for evaluation," I replied. "Outside of that, I'm paying for the ride myself."

The duration of the silence between conversations was awkward and embarrassing. "This is Saturday Night Live material," I thought.

Several minutes passed before Bubba presented another question.

"So how much does a motorcycle like yours *cost,* anyway?" Bubba asked, trying not to sound too interested.

"Oh, about seventeen or eighteen grand, fitted out the way it is," I replied. As the words were passing my lips, I thought about how unlikely it was that any of these guys had ever paid as much for a car. What would they think if they knew I had a carbon copy of the motorcycle sitting in the garage at home, and a third one worth about half as much?

After a while, Ed finally mustered the courage to suggest an idea. It was the type of reaction I would have bet 150 bucks I'd eventually see.

"You know, I think the owner of this pit might keep some gasoline up by his place. I'd check for you, but I guess now that you've called the Chevron station, it's probably a waste of time."

"Not true," I responded. "I have no idea how long it will really take the station to make this service call. If you can get me some fuel even ten minutes earlier, it would be worth it to me."

"I'll go check," Ed responded.

"How far away is the owner's place," I asked, as Ed headed for the door.

"Oh, maybe five minutes. I'll be right back."

Now I imagined that Ed would rush for the gas, wanting to pull it off before the service call could be made from the Alamo service station.

I walked outside to see what effect the rain was having on the parking lot. The rain had been falling hard for some time now, it was dark, and the lot was becoming very slippery. I didn't want to drop the bike in front of these guys, after just making a seemingly preposterous claim of my riding credentials. Rather than returning to the office, I waited for Ed to return with gasoline. The riding suit was keeping me dry and I removed a baseball cap from the tank bag to cover my head.

After a few minutes, four bright lights of Ed's loader appeared from the darkness.

"Got it," Ed smiled as he eased himself down from the loader. "This can has about two and a half gallons in it."

"Now you're sure this isn't diesel," I quipped, thinking once again of the difficulties Manny Samiero caused for himself when he accidentally filled his motorcycle with diesel fuel during the '97 Iron Butt Rally. I opened the filler cap of the motorcycle and pointed to where Ed could pour the gasoline.

"No, it's gasoline all right," Ed responded. He smelled the contents nonetheless before proceeding to pour.

"The owner keeps gasoline for emergencies, but he sure charges a lot for it," Ed remarked as he poured the remainder of the gasoline.

"Well, I hope this covers it," I said, as I handed him a twenty dollar bill. "Here, let me give you a copy of the poop sheet on this ride I'm doing, too," I said as I handed him one of my information sheets. "I'll go back inside to cancel the road service call."

"Yes, this is great," he responded. "Thanks. Don't worry about the road service though. I called from the owner's place as soon as I was sure we had gas here."

Ed seemed more interested in expressing some interest and enthusiasm about my ride, now that he wasn't in the presence of Bubba and the supervisor.

"Listen, I'm a little worried about dropping this bike now that I have to ride through this muddy field to get out of here. I can't even see the road well enough to get out. Would you mind leading the way? If I do drop the motorcycle, I'd like to know that someone is around to help me get it back up."

"No problem," Ed responded. "You head up the trail right over there, and I'll follow you on the loader."

By now, I had come to expect witnesses to wait for my arrival, but it didn't make me feel better about it. It was raining heavily as I continued to Ely. I stopped at the Chevron station in Alamo and filled the tank before continuing. I was scheduled to be in Ely at 11:00 p.m. It was after 9:00 p.m. when I finished refueling in Alamo and I had nearly another 200 miles to ride before reaching Ely. Considering the heavy rain and my state of exhaustion, I knew I was going to be late again.

At about 11:30 p.m., as I was crossing the Oak Springs Summit and approaching Caliente, my Utah witnesses were already meeting at the Best Western Salt Flat Motel in Wendover, Utah, and I had yet to complete the Nevada checkpoint in Ely.

Russell Clegg and his wife Marra had ridden to Wendover from Salt Lake City, just 120 miles to the east. Kyle Sims and Terry Smith each rode more than 600 miles, from Oakland, California, and Whittier, California, respectively. Terry was the last to arrive. When he met the other witnesses, Terry learned that they were expecting me to arrive in about 45 minutes.

"No," Terry informed them. "Ron was due in Ely at 11:00 p.m. I don't think he'll do 120 miles in 75 minutes. I just came through Ely and there's a hell of a thunderstorm all the way up, blowing pouring rain and wind. Besides, he's got 40 miles of construction to ride through."

Kyle also confronted severe weather on his way from San Francisco to Wendover. A few days after riding to Wendover, Kyle wrote to Barbara and the other witnesses with a description of his account. In part, Kyle wrote:

> *I had hightailed it from Oakland, CA, through fog, hail, multiple, scary thunderstorms, and finally 'why, exactly, am I doing this?'-style crosswinds, to arrive in Wendover an hour before Ron's scheduled arrival time, as he requested, so I had a sense of what he might be dealing with as we waited for him.*

When it was about two hours beyond my scheduled arrival time, Bill Miner called Roberta from Ely to see if there was any recent news. It was 3:00 a.m. in Texas, but by this point in my ride, the situation was so intense that riders were less reluctant to place a call at odd hours. Roberta's latest information was based on my departure from Needles, California. Realizing that I was two hours overdue, in a thunderstorm, Roberta pulled out her rosary.

As I was approaching Ely, Ira Agins, one of my New Mexico witnesses, was responding to an e-mail message that Norm Grills had posted to LDRIDER a few hours earlier. Norm had written:

> *I don't know about the rest of you, but I feel like I am on that bike with him. It may be personal to him, but I have made it personal to me. I have followed his progress on his web pages in my waking hours at work and at home. I rode to Texarkana to meet him at midnight on Tuesday, getting back home at 3:30 a.m. and at work for an 8:00 a.m. meeting, but I would do it again in a heartbeat.*

*Those of us fortunate to have shared a few brief
moments with him as he is hopefully making history,
will no doubt feel like we played a small, small part in
helping and encouraging him.*

In his response, Ira wrote:

*It never ceases to amaze me, this Internet. The line
between cyber-reality and physical reality really gets
cloudy sometimes. It's having very-long-range
scanners, knowing almost minute-by-minute where
Ron is and how he's doing. At the checkpoint, Ron
mentioned the repair Paul Glaves made to the turn
signal. Yup, heard about it. The big lightning storm
that had him sidelined for a while? That, too. Indeed,
it is riding along in the most vicarious way, and once
in a while weaving between the cyber and the physical.
And to dream the ride Ron is taking.*

Can't wait for the barbecue. Lots to talk about.

Before my departure four days ago, when preparing the final version of the route sheets to be inserted behind the window
of my tank bag, I tried to abbreviate them as much as possible. I
wanted to reduce the number of sheets I carried, so as to minimize the number of times I would have to remove sheets from
the tank bag to turn to the next page. One of the details I elimi-
nated when I prepared the sheets was the name and address of
the checkpoint location in Ely. When Kim Rydalch first suggested the Chevron station on the main route leading into Ely, I
was confident that I knew exactly where the station was located. I had been through Ely no less than a half-dozen times
during the past three years.

When I arrived, it was almost 1:00 a.m. I entered the town,
realizing I had been mistaken about the location of the Chevron
station. I headed downtown, hoping the station was in that direction, and I became frustrated when I didn't see it. I parked
the motorcycle and prepared to enter the lobby of a nearby hotel
for directions. As I was removing my helmet, a police car
stopped at a traffic signal a few feet from where I stood. I
walked to the patrol car and tried to attract the officer's attention. The light turned green as I reached his car and he began to

drive off. I rapped on his rear fender as the car was pulling away, but he didn't notice me.

When I walked back to the hotel, another patrol car stopped and the officer rolled his window down and asked if he could help.

"I saw you trying to get my buddy's attention. What's the problem?" the officer asked.

"I'm supposed to meet a few friends on motorcycles at a Chevron station somewhere here in Ely. Can you tell me where I can find it?" I asked.

"Sorry," the officer offered as he pulled away.

Just as I was about to enter the hotel, the policeman who I first attempted to flag down pulled to the curb.

"Sorry I didn't stop a few minutes ago. My buddy radioed me to tell me you tried to flag me down."

I repeated my question to the officer.

"Those must be your friends at the Chevron up the road," the officer answered. "I was admiring their motorcycles. Just head up this road a few miles and you'll see them on the left."

I thanked the officer, got back on the motorcycle, and rode to the Chevron station.

Just then, Bill Miner was hanging up after talking to Roberta.

Four riders met me in Ely. Warren Harhay, an executive with a Nevada-based Internet service provider who completed the '97 Iron Butt Rally, was the first of the group to volunteer. Warren rode almost 300 miles from Boulder City, Nevada. Ken Carlton rode more than 200 miles from his home in southwestern Utah. Bill Miner rode nearly 500 miles from Sacramento. Kim Rydalch enlisted his friend, Spencer Whatcott, to ride the 500 miles with him from Modesto, California, on the other side of the Sierra Nevada mountains.

Kim and Spencer used the 7/49 as an excuse for a four-day fun ride around Nevada. Their ride included such attractions as riding beside ten-foot-high walls of snow at the top of 9,628-foot Sonora Pass, exploring Rachel, Nevada, and the Extraterrestrial Highway, and running out of gas two miles from a Chevron station in Baker, Nevada.

Nevada checkpoint: Warren Harhay, Bill Miner, Kim Rydalch, Ron, and Ken Carlton.

While I was still in the process of getting signatures, Bill called Roberta to tell her of my safe arrival. Roberta immediately called Russell Clegg at the motel in Wendover and reported that I had been delayed when I ran out of gas, but that I had arrived in Ely safely although behind schedule.

Day	State	Miles Ridden	Miles to Go
6	44	6,848	1,950

The most difficult hours of my seven-day ride were those spent between Ely, Nevada, and Wendover, Utah. They were also the most dangerous three hours of the trip. The anxiety and delay caused by nearly running out of fuel near Alamo, the pounding rain, and the fact that I had rested less than one hour in the last 24 was weighing very heavily on me when I pulled away from the gasoline pumps in Ely. I was tired and craving sleep. I wanted to be in Wendover. I wanted to be in a warm bed. There are times when 120 miles pass very quickly. At other times, the miles can seem endless. Tonight, they would seem endless and lonely.

I was so exhausted that I felt I had gone beyond the point of being safe. Even though I knew witnesses were waiting for me in Wendover, I wanted to stop for at least a thirty-minute nap, but there were no rest areas. Lages Station is halfway between Ely and Wendover, at the junction where Route 93 continues north to Wells and Alternate Route 93 veers to the northeast to Utah. I remembered the stop from other trips, but couldn't remember if there was a place to rest. I hoped I would find a covered picnic table when I arrived.

When I reached Lages Station, the café was closed and there was no place to sleep. The ground was wet and muddy, so I stopped in the parking lot, placed the motorcycle on the centerstand, and lay forward across my tank bag to sleep. As tired as I was, I was unable to sleep in that position. After less than ten minutes, I started the motorcycle and continued. I only had another 60 miles to travel before I could sleep in a warm bed and then start the final push to capture Idaho, Oregon, and Washington to complete the 48-state ride.

No more than ten miles had passed before I was having difficulty maintaining my speed, keeping my eyes open, and keeping the bike on the road. I decided I would have to stop again and make another attempt at napping. When I pulled to the shoulder, the earth was so soft from the rain that I couldn't place the bike on its sidestand for fear it would fall over. The ground was also too soft for me to be able to get the bike up on the centerstand. When I tried, the centerstand sank quickly into the soft earth and the bike started to go over. I considered leaving the bike on the desolate roadway until I could find a rock to place beneath the sidestand. At that moment, I was passed by one of the few vehicles I encountered on the highway that evening. I decided that rather than nap, I would park the bike on the roadway and do calisthenics to refresh me enough to ride the remaining 50 miles or so. I performed jumping jacks and some deep knee bends, then continued on.

In spite of all the discomfort I was suffering, I was happy that the First Gear riding suit was performing as well as Paul

Golde had assured me it would. I was absolutely dry, as I had been during the thunderstorms in Oklahoma and Minnesota.

I tried all of the tricks I knew to stay awake: Cursing, singing, shaking my head, standing on the foot pegs—it didn't help much. I left the face shield of my helmet open, hoping it would help to keep me alert; rain pellets stung my face, but I still struggled to stay awake.

The only other thing that I could possibly have done would have been to park the motorcycle and hitch a ride to Wendover with whoever eventually may have decided to stop for me. But there wasn't a place to leave the motorcycle. And I didn't want to abandon my goal.

I've frequently been asked to speak before groups about motorcycle endurance riding. A question about safety is always asked, and my response is always the same.

"When you leave your house to ride in an automobile, you are subjecting yourself to a little more risk than if you stay home. If you travel by motorcycle instead of by car, the risk increases. If you ride after dark or in the rain, or ride faster than your skills and abilities warrant, risk increases still more. If you also ride when you're tired, you are taking even more risk.

"Many people think riding a motorcycle is too risky under any circumstances. But for those who choose to ride, the question becomes, 'where do you wish to place yourself on the risk scale?' Those who are *competitive* about endurance riding expose themselves to more risk than most riders do.

"I'm considered a risk-taker, in both my business life and my personal life. But whether in business or in endurance riding, the risks I take are calculated and deliberate, not reckless, or accidental. And I do all I can reasonably do to mitigate them.

"I ride safe, well-maintained motorcycles, and always wear protective clothing. I've taken advanced training and frequently practice my skills. I never ride after drinking and I avoid riding in populated areas on Saturday nights when, statistically at least, a high percentage of motorists are legally drunk. I stop to rest when I'm too tired to ride safely.

"I know a few riders who are so incompetent they shouldn't compete in endurance events. But most experienced endurance riders mitigate the risks through superior riding skills and safe practices, and are therefore less likely to harm themselves."

I knew the script. But late this rainy night in Nevada, I was disregarding my own dictum about stopping when too tired to ride safely. I was pushing the edge of the envelope and it was bulging at the seams, threatening to tear. I didn't like doing this, but I didn't know what else to do.

Route 93 between Ely and Wendover has always been one of my favorite roads. Every time I've ridden it, I've felt there is something mystical about it. Riding the road has always made me think how fortunate I am to have discovered motorcycles, and especially to have discovered endurance riding. I once told Barbara that if the sport killed me, I'd like to be cremated and have my ashes cast to the wind by a motorcyclist riding 100 mph on that route, from a spot overlooking the Great Salt Lake Desert in neighboring Utah. How ironic that I was pushing my limits on the one highway, of all the highways in the world, where I had talked of having my ashes spread.

In all of my endurance riding, I can only recall one occasion when I allowed myself to become so tired that I actually rode the bike onto the shoulder of the road. It happened during my first endurance event, the 1995 Iron Butt Rally. That time, I headed directly for the next motel for four hours of sleep.

Although I didn't run the motorcycle off the road this time, I suddenly found myself in the oncoming lane of traffic, about to leave the roadway for the left shoulder. That got my adrenaline flowing and my heart beating rapidly.

Few of us have ever stood in the wind on the outside ledge of a towering skyscraper, sixty stories up, looking down at the street, feeling that we've just lost our balance and are about to fall forward. Think about it. That's what it's like to unexpectedly find that you're about to leave the road at 70 mph on a dark night in heavy rain on a motorcycle.

As I steered the bike back into the right lane, I could see the distant lights of the casinos in Wendover.

Utah checkpoint: Kyle Sims, Terry Smith, Russell Clegg, Marra Clegg, and Ron.

45 - Utah

Wendover, like Texarkana, straddles two states. I first visited Wendover, Nevada, in 1996 while participating in the Utah 1088, but I hadn't been into town on the Utah side. The sight of lights and the knowledge that I would soon be able to stop and sleep for several hours heartened and sustained me until I finally reached Wendover. My witnesses were waiting faithfully in the parking lot.

"How are you *really* doing?" Terry Smith asked, as I was removing the earplugs.

"I'm having the time of my life," I responded. It wasn't difficult to come up with such a positive response, now only a few hundred feet away from a bed and with only three more states and less than 600 miles to go before completing the 48-state ride. Although I was behind schedule, I was well within striking distance of the record.

I apologized for causing my friends to have to stay up so late due to my tardiness.

"No problem, Ron," Terry answered. "You have a lot of friends who want to see you make it." Then he replenished my supply of bananas.

The motel had already closed for the night, but I had made a guaranteed reservation. My witnesses had obtained the key to my room so I could avoid the check-in process.

Knowing I would be starting the final leg of my ride after the next few hours of sleep, I skipped the shower and headed straight to bed. Before turning in, I removed the route slips from the top of my tank bag and wrote "UTAH GAS" in large letters across the form. I wanted to be sure not to forget to fill the tank before leaving for Idaho in the morning.

"Don't forget to lock that top box before you take off in the morning," Terry quipped, as Kyle and I headed for our rooms.

It would be nearly a week later before I would read about Kyle's opinion of my status in his message to Barbara and the other witnesses. Kyle's words were very flattering and quite surprising to me when I recall my fatigue during the ride from Ely to Wendover. Kyle wrote:

I had never met Ron before, and was both amazed, and not, to see the impish sparkle in his eye, and to be engaged by his quick wit at this ungodly hour after all that he had endured.

After all, who better suited to undertake a 7/49 ride? Why should I have been amazed? Yes, he looked tired, but who wouldn't? I observed that, basically, Ron was alert, focused, and capable.

Terry had managed to nap while waiting for me. He was so jazzed up about being part of the event that he headed for home via the same route I had just taken from Ely. He later told me that when he was about halfway to Ely, the sun came up and he enjoyed a magnificent view. There were mountains on both sides of the highway; the Egan Range to the west and the Creek Range to the east. The clouds were sitting low and engulfed a good portion of the mountains. Below the clouds on each side of the highway was a herd of elk.

Despite my exhausted state, I awoke several minutes before the Screaming Meanie sounded. At first I thought the telephone had awakened me. The phone either rang, or I dreamed
that it had, but in either case, I was spared the agony of having
to locate and disarm the scream machine.

After filling up with gas at a Utah service station, I headed
for the Boise checkpoint. It was a gorgeous morning and I could-
n't have felt better as I entered the ramp for I-80 and points
west. I now had less than 600 miles to go for the 48-state record.

Day	State	Miles Ridden	Miles to Go
6	45	6,972	1,826

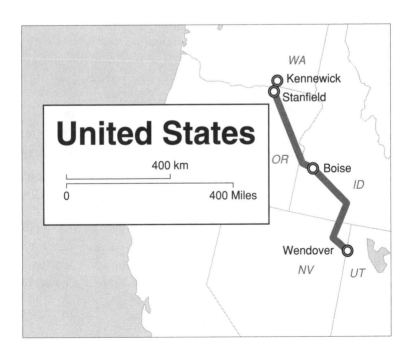

9

Utah to Washington

As I was preparing to leave Utah for the Idaho checkpoint, Dale Wilson was posting a message to LDRIDER:

Maggots!!

While much to-do has been justifiably made about the 7/49, Ron is about to break another record a few hours from now: the Mike Kneebone/Fran Crane record of 48-states in six days.

If he stays on schedule, Ron should beat the original 6 days, 13 hours, and 21 minutes record by about half a day!

The Columbia Basin is broiling today. Crystal-clear skies and a searing sun. When Ron comes down off the High Plateau of northeastern Oregon, he'll think he's back in the Nevada desert!

The moment he crosses the border and we sign his forms to stop the clock, we'll lead him to Crocodile Motor Sports for the tire change/oil change/CB antenna repair.

Then . . . north, to Alaska! This is almighty exciting!

Will try to take a couple quick Polaroid photos of Ron for the IBA/MERA web sites.

Dale

A little later, as I was riding through Nevada on my way to Idaho, Steve Wilson, one of my witnesses from Ruston, Louisiana, posted the following:

I am in awe of your attempt. It makes those 12-hour days in a yellow seat seem much shorter now. I am the guy that told you about our Ruston peaches. If you will e-mail me back a street address (if you ever get back to Plano) I would be honored to send a case of the best peaches you ever ate.

As of this writing, you haven't made it to Alaska yet, but congratulations in advance. By the time you read this I'm sure you will have.

P.S.: You may be the toughest man alive, but the lady in Plano is stronger. Congratulations to her as well.

Steve Wilson

After leaving Wendover, I didn't stop again until I reached Jackpot, Nevada, near the border between Nevada and Idaho. Jackpot is typical of many Nevada border towns. Driving south on Route 93, Jackpot is the first opportunity for visitors from the north to contribute to the Nevada economy.

I refueled and pointed the bike toward the Idaho border. Barbara was scheduled to arrive in Terrace, British Columbia, at about this time. From there she would rent a car and drive to Hyder to await my arrival.

When Barbara arrived at the airport in Terrace, she called Roberta to determine if there had been additional news of my progress. Roberta told her about having been awakened earlier in the morning by the Nevada witnesses, about retrieving her rosary, and about receiving word from Bill Miner a few minutes later.

When Roberta told Barbara that I had nearly run out of gas in Nevada, they were concerned I was starting to make dumb mistakes and the lack of sleep was taking its toll. If they had known that I had actually had the forethought *not* to run out of gas in the middle of the Nevada desert, perhaps they wouldn't have been as concerned.

Barbara and Roberta talked so long about the events that had transpired that the girl who had come from town with the rental car returned to town. Barbara had to call her to return to the airport.

46 - Idaho

Bob Ward had departed his home in Bonney Lake, Washington, for Boise on Friday morning. He used the occasion as an excuse to take a vacation day to ride his Kawasaki Concours 500 miles to Boise. When he arrived in Boise, he checked into a motel close to the checkpoint, had dinner, then rode to the Flying J Truck Stop that I had selected as the checkpoint. The truck stop was located three quarters of a mile from the highway exit. Bob noted that access from the highway wasn't so great and a trip inside the station would be required to secure a receipt. Bob knew that Randall Weers and Michael Gasper would be arriving to meet me, too, and decided to discuss changing the checkpoint location.

When Bob, Michael, and Randall met for breakfast in the morning, they decided to intercept me on the way to the checkpoint and escort me to a Chevron station ten miles further west. The trio selected a lookout point east of Boise where they could survey traffic heading west. They positioned themselves on an overpass 45 minutes before I was expected to arrive. While they waited, Bob and Michael naughtily entertained themselves by pointing a small, rolled-up rain suit at traffic below. Drivers, thinking the volunteers were police officers with a radar unit, slowed as they approached.

When I arrived I saw the riders and recognized Michael's Gold Wing. Even with my broken CB antenna, I recognized Michael's voice informing me that the trio had selected an alternate checkpoint. After riding with me to the Idaho checkpoint, the three riders would accompany me to Oregon and finally to the end of the 48-state ride in Washington.

When I arrived at the checkpoint, I discovered that one of the screws securing my right luggage case to the motorcycle was missing. I would have to repair it before continuing, especially if I was going to ride all the way to Alaska after finishing the 48-state portion of the trip.

Randall Weers, who was also riding a K1100LT, quickly removed the bolt from his own motorcycle and used it to repair mine. The swap required only a few minutes and we were on our way to Oregon.

Leaving Boise, we skirted the eastern edge of the High Cascades and climbed onto the Columbia Plateau, an upland region located between the Rocky Mountains and the Cascade Range. We crossed Deadmans Pass and descended from the Blue Mountains to Pendleton, where Fran Crane and Mike Kneebone had started their 48-state ride ten years earlier.

Day	State	Miles Ridden	Miles to Go
6	46	7,276	1,522

47 - Oregon

Jeff Earls and John Bowne departed the Portland area a little after 8:00 a.m. and had arrived at Buffalo Junction three hours later. Dale Wilson and Joe Zulaski joined them briefly to insure things were in order, then returned to the Washington checkpoint to wait for me. John O'Keefe, Kerry Church, John Cheney, and Scott Larson arrived a little later.

A dedicated endurance riding enthusiast, Jeff is entered in the 1999 Iron Butt Rally. He had already completed numerous rallies of shorter duration and was co-Rallymaster, with Keith Underdahl, of the Timberbutt. Jeff also races motorcycles and is a Senior Instructor for the Motorcycle Safety Foundation.

Jeff went ahead to the Stanfield exit to inform the manager of the station what was happening and to ask permission to block a pump for a few minutes before the scheduled arrival. The manager readily agreed, and Kerry Church parked his Gold Wing in front of a pump.

As my journey progressed, the effect it was having on other riders was becoming increasingly obvious to me. But I had no idea that Jerry Harris, one of the riders who accompanied me from Santa Fe to Albuquerque just the day before, would already be starting his first 1,000-mile day because of the inspiration my ride had generated.

Since meeting me, Jerry hadn't been able to stop thinking about long rides. The tires on his BMW were marginal for a long ride, but he also owned a new Harley-Davidson with fewer than a thousand miles on the odometer. Jerry downloaded the forms for completing a SaddleSore 1000 from the Iron Butt web site, visited Chick's Harley-Davidson for witnesses, and departed at 3:00 p.m.—about the time I was entering the Oregon checkpoint. Jerry then rode through Grand Junction, to Denver, and back down I-25 to Albuquerque to successfully complete his first 1,000-mile day.

At about 2:00 p.m., Bryce Ulrich and his friend Marie Grohman arrived at the Buffalo Junction checkpoint. They informed the other riders that Michael Gasper was escorting me to Oregon and would use the truck stop in Stanfield, rather than the dusty and dilapidated Buffalo Junction location I had selected. Michael had called Bryce to report that he should expect us in Stanfield at 3:15 p.m.

Bryce is a software developer who recently left Microsoft to take a year to ride his motorcycle around the country. He and Marie had departed the Seattle area early in the morning with a half-dozen other riders to make the 600-mile ride to greet me in Oregon and Washington. Marie, a family practice physician, had fashioned a large "7/49" sign and attached it to the rear of Bryce's motorcycle. The couple stationed themselves beside the road a few miles before Buffalo Junction to lead the way to the new Oregon checkpoint.

"When Marie and I were waiting to provide escort service to the Oregon checkpoint, we got goose bumps as we first saw one headlight, then another, and then about a half dozen-flying down the hill toward us," Bryce related. Marie even let out a squeal! I started the bike and made my way down the freeway ramp as quickly as I could and pulled in front of the group."

I developed goose bumps, too. Being accompanied by so many friends, and seeing how much so many other riders were getting into my ride was very inspiring.

I arrived at the checkpoint at 3:10 p.m. and was on my way at 3:17 p.m. Since I had already purchased gasoline in Oregon, it wasn't necessary to refuel.

Day	State	Miles Ridden	Miles to Go
6	47	7,511	1,287

Meanwhile, Barbara was entering Hyder, looking for the Sealaska Inn. As she passed the Glacier Inn Bar on her way down the unpaved street, she was pleasantly surprised to see a large banner spread across the front of the building: "Congratulations Ron Ayres." As she approached the Sealaska Inn, she saw Don Moses on his Gold Wing, looking for a public phone in Hyder that was operable.

"Wait until I check into my room. You can use my phone," Barbara offered.

"You think you've got a phone in your room," Don smirked sarcastically. "The public phone here at the hotel doesn't work and cell phones don't work in Hyder."

When Barbara parked the car and looked for the hotel office, she came upon Tracy DesLaurier and Herb Anderson. She learned she wouldn't be able to check in until 5:00 p.m. when the bar opened, as the bar also served as the hotel desk.

When Don returned from his unsuccessful attempt to reach the outside world, the four of them walked to a quaint, little one-room restaurant called The Border Café for lunch. The owner amused the group with stories of bears that sometimes walk the streets of Hyder, including one who once tried to enter her café from the back door.

Caroline Gutierrez entered the café and joined them.

I was surprised when, at least a year before my ride, Caroline filled out the volunteer form on my web site. When I saw her Hyder address, I first thought it was a prank. I knew the population of Hyder was fewer than 150 people, and I never would have expected one of the town's residents to discover my web site. Caroline discovered my site when she had searched on the Internet to see what had been published about her home town. She was as surprised to learn I would be using the town for the terminus of my ride as I was to learn I would have a genuine Hyder witness waiting for me. During the next year, Caroline would prove to be an invaluable source of information about the area.

In the late 60s, Caroline's parents had become pessimistic about the country's future, fearing an economic collapse and another Great Depression. In 1972, they decided to sell everything and go where they could "live off the land."

"Hyder seemed perfect," Caroline says. "Far enough north that no one in their right mind would want to live here, far enough south that it was possible to live off the land, and in an area not likely to be radically impacted by growth or change.

"My days were spent wrapped around the wood stove, and my nights weren't much better. We slept in an attic room that was divided in half by cardboard boxes. Even with flannel sheets, wool blankets, quilted, nylon-shelled long johns, and full-length, sheep-skin coats, we shivered all night long. In addition, each night before bed, Mom would force me, my sister, and my two brothers to drink a big glass of water. When we would finally get to sleep, the water we drank would force us to get up.

"Mom's plan was simple, but effective. As each of us made a trip to the bathroom, we would add a piece of wood to the fire. This not only kept the fire going, but kept the pipes from freezing up, as we used the bathroom."

When there was neither an economic collapse nor another depression, Caroline's family eventually sold their secreted stash of gold, ate their two-year supply of groceries, and moved on. Only Caroline and one of her brothers remained in Hyder.

When Caroline joined the group in the café, she reported that she had been following my progress on the Internet and related how Gary Dehner's message about watching his son follow me into the night from the Kentucky checkpoint had brought tears to her eyes.

Since Don hadn't been able to place a phone call to check on my progress, he composed a message to Dale Wilson, which Caroline sent via e-mail.

As Barbara, Tracy, Herb, and Don were walking the streets of Hyder, Chris Baldwin arrived. A corporate lawyer in Vancouver, Chris participated with me in the Alberta 2000 in 1997 and is entered in the Iron Butt in 1999. When told about the problem with the phones, Chris rode to nearby Stewart, Canada, to try to make a phone call. The quartet continued on to the Canadian Customs station at the border to see if the customs official would permit them to use their phone.

The group was not successful in placing a credit card call from the customs station, but the agent on duty encouraged them to dial direct, compliments of the Canadian government. Canadians Tracy and Herb were amused and pleased to see some of their tax money used to support such a worthy cause.

Barbara asked Dale Wilson's wife, Kathy, to post a message to let the community know the group was *incommunicado* and might not be able to let people know of my arrival.

48 - Washington At Last

Riding the final twenty miles or so from Stanfield to the Washington border, I experienced an incredible feeling of personal satisfaction. I knew I was about to break the ten-year-old, 48-state record in nearly the "under six days" I had set as a target. Although I intended to proceed to Alaska after the stop in Washington, completing 49 states in less than seven days would be frosting on the cake. It wasn't nearly as important as beating the widely acclaimed 48-state record.

As we approached the DOT truck weigh station, riders who had been in front of me slowed and waved me around so that I would be first in the entourage to pass through the gates at the station. There were at least a few dozen riders waiting with Dale Wilson. As soon as I stopped, a man and woman approached me, offered their congratulations, and introduced themselves as staff members for *Easyriders* magazine. Michael Gasper presented me with a "Big Dog" tee shirt with an illustration of dogs riding motorcycles.

I opened the trunk case for the 48th time in six days, removed the binder, unzipped the cover, removed one of the pens, and passed it to Dale.

Witnesses sign the forms in Kennewick, Washington (photo by Bryce Ulrich).

"That's OK," Dale responded, as he withdrew his own pen from his jacket. "I'm going to sign for the 48-state record with my own pen, then I want you to have it."

As Dale passed his pen to me, I noted that it was inscribed with a special message about the importance of teamwork. I remarked on the appropriateness of the slogan and thanked him for his thoughtfulness in providing the memento. I placed it inside my riding suit for safekeeping.

I chuckled to myself as I thought about the way my collection of pens had changed during my ride. Before I started, I had placed four new, matching ballpoint pens into the front of the binder. The collection of pens changed as my ride progressed. At one of the stops, the binder contained an expensive Cross pen. I made a mental note to remove it in case its owner later asked about it. Several stops later, the Cross had disappeared and a different pen appeared in its place. Now, near the end of my ride, none of my original four pens were in the collection.

Dale recorded the time of 15:38 PST on the witness form. That equated to 18:38 EST. My 48-state ride was made in six days and twelve minutes! I made it!

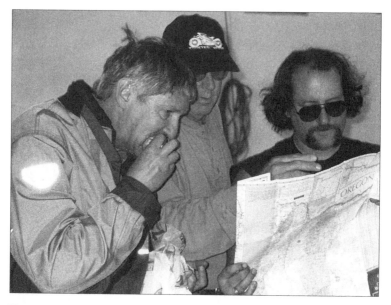

Ron eats a tuna sub at Crocodile Motorsports while Dale Wilson
helps with the map (photo by Bryce Ulrich).

After securing Ron Smith's signature, Dale instructed me
to follow him to Crocodile Motorsports for the new tire, oil
change, and antenna repair. 1997 Iron Butt veteran Tom Loftus
was on hand for witness duty, too. He assured me he would follow us to the shop and complete the signing there.

Before leaving the weigh station I signed the witness forms
for Jeffery Foster, who had started from the Santa Fe checkpoint, and who finished his 1,500 mile, 24-hour ride at my
Washington checkpoint.

As Dale and I approached the dealership in Kennewick, I
remembered that I had neglected to secure signatures of the
DOT officials working the weigh station. When we stopped for a
traffic signal, I pulled beside him, opened my face shield, and
signaled that I wanted to speak to him.

"What about the police officer signatures," I shouted to Dale
as he lifted the visor on his helmet.

I could tell from the expression on Dale's face that he had
forgotten about the original purpose in selecting the DOT station. It wasn't Dale's fault that I departed the station without

Ron is crowned "Top Banana" (photo by Bryce Ulrich).

the police signatures, but I could tell from his expression that he felt responsible, after planning a perfect 48th-state reception.

"That's all right," Dale shouted. "When we reach the shop, I'll call for a police cruiser to stop by."

When Dale was planning the final checkpoint for me, I had asked him what we would do about police signatures in the event the DOT station was closed when I arrived. Dale decided we would call for a police cruiser. Although I felt that we could work it out, I was concerned that the official ending time would be the time that the police officers signed the form. Although I had beat the previous record by a significant margin, I regretted that I was possibly losing time for later police signatures.

When we reached the shop, owner Jack Baird had cleared the way in anticipation of my arrival. My motorcycle was placed on the lift and was in the air less than a minute after I arrived. As soon as I had dismounted, Jack offered to provide a place where I could nap while the motorcycle was being serviced. In anticipation of me requiring some sleep before continuing to Alaska, Jack brought a mattress to the shop and prepared a darkened office.

"Thanks anyway," I responded. "I'm not tired enough to nap at the moment, and I'd like to get going as soon as possible." I was so excited about having broken the record that sleep at this point wouldn't have been possible.

Dale placed a call to the police and requested the cruiser. I retrieved a copy of the rules to verify that police signatures were required at the finish.

"Dale, according to the official rules, if police signatures aren't available, signatures of four members of the IBA may be used, so long as I provide an explanation as to why police signatures were not provided. Fortunately, I have the four signatures, so I suppose the IBA will accept it."

"Great," "Dale responded. I've called the cruiser anyway, and I'll personally explain to Mike Kneebone about the final checkpoint. I'm sure it will be fine."

Joe Zulaski walked into the shop, carrying a large, tuna fish submarine sandwich. He had contacted Barbara to ask me what I wanted. When he got his answer, he wrote to the Internet community:

Take note, Ron's asked for a tuna fish sandwich (I think he's finally had his fill of bananas). It only took 47 states and 10,000 pounds of bananas. Ron's new nickname should be "King Kong" for more reasons than just the bananas.

Ira Agins responded:

No, I think from this time forward, Ron is known as the Top Banana.

"What the heck is all this," Mark Reis said as he extracted the wiring for my CB radio from the front fairing of the motorcycle. "Who installed this thing?" Mark exclaimed in disgust.

"Wait a minute, what are you even doing in there," I asked, in surprise. "I thought you were going to install a new antenna on the motorcycle."

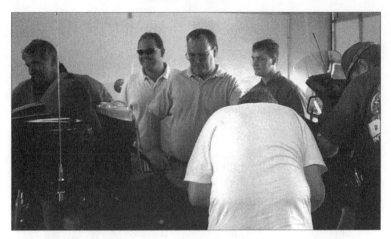

Ron's motorcycle gets serviced at Crocodile Motorsports (photo by
Bryce Ulrich).

"Now Mark, this isn't the time to reengineer anything," Ron
Smith interjected. "Let's just get the man back on the road."

I'm not an electronics wizard, but I knew the installation of
my CB radio was done poorly. I also knew of Mark's reputation
as an electronics wizard. But the thought of spending time to fix
it at this point seemed pointless and unnecessary. I didn't want
to embarrass or insult someone who had gone out of his way to
help me, but I didn't want to let the situation get out of control
and use more time than was necessary to replace the antenna.

"Mark, I appreciate what you're doing," I said. "I wish I had
time for you to fix the system properly, but if I had to choose between taking ten minutes to fix it, or leaving the entire radio
laying here on the floor, I'd tell you to just rip the thing out and
leave it here. I don't have time to fix something that is so unim-
portant to finishing the trip."

Dale approached and asked me some inapposite question. I
hesitated for a moment to be sure I heard Dale correctly. I was
tired and suspected that I may have misunderstood the question, but the question was so irrelevant that I was confused.

"Why did you ask such a question?" I asked.

"To keep you distracted," Dale smiled.

Responding to my anxiety, Mark quickly replaced the spa-
ghetti wiring and prepared to get me on my way. He remarked

Jack Baird is the owner of Crocodile Motorsports, where Ron had his
motorcycle serviced before heading for Hyder.

that he would love to get his hands on the motorcycle to rein-
stall the unit properly. I committed to deliver the motorcycle to
him in Seattle some time in the future.

"What do I owe you?" I asked Jack as my motorcycle was being rolled off the lift and into the parking lot.

"You don't owe me anything," he answered.

Jack had been a long-distance enthusiast for his entire
motorcycling career. He had heard about the Iron Butt Association while working in Los Angeles for NBC TV. It wasn't until
years later when he moved to Kennewick and met Dale Wilson
that he had an opportunity to get involved in Iron Butt events.
Jack now plans to ride the Iron Butt Rally in 2001.

Jack had ridden more than 130 miles to the nearest BMW
dealership to be sure that he serviced my motorcycle properly.
He didn't want to take any chances on screwing up by not using
the correct torque to tighten lug nuts or by overlooking some
important service requirement.

I thanked him for the great job his shop performed, and discussed the continuation of my trip with Dale. I told Dale that I

would like to stop at a nearby station to fill my tank before proceeding to the Canadian border.

"Fine," Dale responded. "After getting the gas, follow me
back to the Interstate. Then Gasper will lead the way to Seattle
and get you set up for your ride north."

Day	State	Miles Ridden	Miles to Go
6	48	7,533	1,265

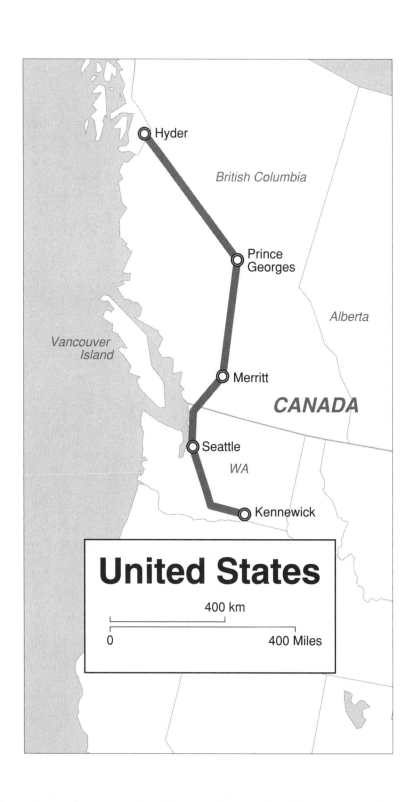

Hyder

British Columbia

Prince
Georges

Alberta

Vancouver
Island

Merritt

CANADA

Seattle

WA

Kennewick

United States

400 km

0   400 Miles

10

Washington to Alaska

I followed Dale to the highway, then fell in behind Michael Gasper as we headed for Seattle. Joe Zulaski and Randall Weers brought up the rear. The cross winds were so strong that I felt that the motorcycle was leaning at a 45-degree angle to compensate.

When we stopped for fuel at Cle Elum, Joe Zulaski bade me farewell and wished me luck with the remainder of the ride, stating that he would be leaving us when we reached Seattle.

As we approached Seattle, I saw Kerry Church sitting beside the road, waiting for us to pass. With his white beard, red

Ron saw Kerry Church, aka Santa Clause, on his way to the Canadian border.

Aerostich, and red Gold Wing, I recall thinking how much he looked like the Santa Claus caricatures on motorcycle-oriented Christmas cards. Randall left us when we reached the I-405 and I-90 interchange, and Joe exited shortly after that. Kerry Church soon passed Michael and me, taking the lead to escort me to the Canadian border crossing at Sumas, knowing that Michael would be taking an exit soon.

Joe Zulaski posted his account of the day as soon as he arrived home:

> OK, the last time I saw Ron and Psycho Mikey, they were burning miles up pretty fast right on I-405 East of North Seattle. This was around 7:45 p.m. Mike is going to lead Ron up to I-5 and then "turn him loose."

> Ron was in great spirits and was joking around. Yes, we did manage to get him his tuna fish sandwich, a foot-long one as I recall. His immediate comment was, "what are you guys trying to do, put me to sleep?" Well, we thought that was the idea, but since Ron was running slightly behind time-wise, he skipped the power nap (and half the sandwich).

> At the truck-stop checkpoint (prior to Ron's arrival), there were a bunch of truckers hanging around getting their vehicles inspected. They all became curious about what was up. After explaining, they proceeded to get their cameras out and hung out with us. Turns out, one of the ladies there was a freelance journalist for Easyriders magazine. She proceeded to take pictures of all us clowns (Dale with his trademark middle finger should play well in Easyriders). Then, pictures galore of Ron when he pulled in. So, get your copies of Easyriders reserved early.

> Oh, a funny side note: Some trucker and his significant other did not join the party, as the driver didn't want his woman going around all those "bikers." First time I've ever been called a biker. Had us all in "stiches" (pun intended).

> OK, so Dale puts me in charge of his camera. I also brought my video camera and a 35mm. So, here I am with all these things hanging off my neck and arms

when Ron pulls in. Plus, our Easyriders *reporter and about 16 other riders (Bryce Ulrich, Dale Wilson, Tom Loftus, Ron Smith, Rody Martin, Mark Reis, Mike Gasper, and a whole lot more). Did I get the video of him riding in? Uhnnnnn! Nope, I spaced it. I was so excited, and everyone was clapping and slapping him on the back that I totally forgot. I did manage to snap a few pictures for Dale but I totally forgot about my own cameras until the last minute.*

Barb, I'll send what video I did get, but it's not much.

Well, the ride to Seattle was fun, fast, and very windy. We all commented about the side bursts and gusts that pummeled us for about 100 miles. Eastern Washington can get pretty windy at times. We all made it through fine, however.

Ron, good luck on the last state and thanks for letting me (for one) share this momentous moment with you.

Joe Zulaski

After the news of my success with the 48-state record, my son Brad amused the readers of my web site with the following announcement:

We are receiving e-mail and phone calls at a geometric rate. I have updated this web site 3 times in 2 hours. We are trying to keep up. We are still waiting for a much-anticipated e-mail from Dale Wilson. His wife called to let us know that they are having communication difficulties from "up there." When we get any news you will be the first to know.

*I don't know about the rest of you, but I am going to celebrate tonight. I am **not** having the party at my apartment. Thank God my dad is most decidedly "out-of-town."*

Brad Ayres

While Kerry and I were heading north on I-5 for the Canadian border, subscribers to LDRIDER were reading Dale's account of events at the Washington checkpoint.

Maggots!

I am pleased to report that, pending IBA verification, Ron Ayres appears to have shattered the mark set by Michael Kneebone and Fran Crane for the run!

According to his rally time upon his arrival at the Washington Checkpoint, Ron's time appears to have been exactly 6 days, 0 hours and 5 minutes!!!!!!!!!!

Unfortunately, the Kennewick Police Department proved uncooperative regarding witness signatures. However, there were plenty of official IBA members on hand to sign as witnesses. In accordance with established Iron Butt rules for the attempt, we obtained the necessary four signatures in lieu of police officers: Ron Smith, Steve Jewett, 1997 IBR 8th place finisher Tom Loftus, and me . . .

The maintenance activities went smoother than I could have hoped. I worked out every detail with Crocodile Motor Sports beforehand, and they had their varsity team of mechanics standing by. Ron rolled up to the driveway, into the shop garage, and immediately up onto the hydraulic lift. He was barely off the bike when the mechanics leaped on it like a pit crew from the Indianapolis 500! The tire was off in 3 minutes, and the oil was draining shortly thereafter.

Ron Smith brought in electrical craftsman Mark Reis, an ECM tech of Ron Major-like caliber, who immediately jumped on Ron's broken CB antenna. He had the right side of Ron's cockpit all ripped out as he hunted down a culprit electrical component, then fine-tuned a new CB antenna with all kinds of electronic meters and oscilloscopes. As he started to explain the phenomenon of Digitally Multiplexed Transmission Scatter as it relates to Aperture-to-Medium Coupling Loss, Ron's eyeballs completely glazed over and he said: "I'm not sure what that means, but I am sure you are correct!!!"

This was an incredibly humorous statement coming from this exhausted man!!!! You had to be there, but trust me, it was a riot!!!!!

*Time between roll-in and roll-out at Crocodile Motor
Sports: 43 minutes. I led Ron out of Crocodile to a
nearby Exxon with Psycho Mikey tucked in behind
him. We topped off his tank, and I led everyone back to
the Interstate. I led Ron north and west toward the
Hanford Nuclear Site, where I gave him a heart-felt
salute as I departed the pattern for home.*

*Ron is fairly well fatigued, but after carefully and
closely observing him as we rode to Kennewick, and
then throughout the maintenance evolution, I can
report to you that he is certainly cognizant of his
condition and is making adjustments as necessary. He
is still quite safe and steady on the road, and he had
no problems maintaining a sub-Nevada pace
throughout our ride together . . .*

Dale

As I was approaching the Canadian border, Barbara, Don
Moses, Herb Anderson, and Tracy DesLaurier were returning
to Hyder from Stewart where they had gone for dinner. They
stopped at the Sealaska Inn bar and sent Don Moses inside to
invite Chris Baldwin to join them for a few beers at the Glacier
Inn.

Barbara later related the events of the evening:

"When Don returned to the car he was holding a copy of
Dale Wilson's LDRIDER announcement that had been sent to
Caroline who delivered it to the bar. We all sat in the enclosed
car, a soft rain falling outside, while Don read the e-mail, almost breathlessly. As he continued to read about Ron breaking
the 48-state record, his voice kept getting higher and higher.
We were all elated. You'd think Ron's achievement had been a
personal achievement for all of us. It was like our team had
won."

The group went to the Glacier Bar and Barbara offered to
buy everyone a beer in my honor. Barbara ordered a Canadian
Ale, a brand she had discovered and enjoyed while in Vancouver.

"We only have American beers," the bartender responded.

Somewhat chagrined, realizing she was now in the United States (although literally within sight of the Canadian border), she ordered a domestic beer instead, and attempted to pay with a $20 bill.

"Oh, we only take Canadian money," the bartender grumbled.

As the group entered the bar, they noticed that the large sign welcoming me to Hyder had been partly torn off. Don, sounding somewhat stern, asked the bartender what had happened to the sign. The bartender explained that his brother worked at the other bar in town and that they were rivals. Apparently, his brother had torn part of the sign down. Don insisted that it be replaced and the bartender assured Don that it would be put back up. By the time they left the bar, there were new signs at *both* of the bars.

My last fuel stop in the United States was at Mount Vernon, Washington. I had delayed replacing my tinted face shield with my clear one until I had to stop for fuel. It was almost 9:00 p.m. when I stopped, and I used the occasion to put on some warmer clothes too, in anticipation of colder temperatures now that the sun was down.

In the meantime, Norm and Linda Babcock had made it to the Meziadin Junction, the last stop where they would be able to obtain fuel before arriving in Hyder. As they were debating the merits of checking into a motel or continuing, Rick Morrison arrived at the station. Rick's motorcycle was equipped with an auxiliary fuel cell and he offered to serve as a "tanker" for Norm and Linda. The trio ran through the late-evening fog toward Hyder. Rick commented about the experience later:

"I was riding ahead of the Babcocks and was first to slice into the fog. It hovered over the road, rising no more than three to four feet. This allowed my headlight to skim the top of it. This gave me an illusion of flying on top of the road—like I would imagine being in an open-cockpit airplane. A very nice memory indeed."

Norm remembered the event from a different perspective:

"Rick set a torrid pace, considering the weather and animal situation. The rain turned to snow, and our visors soon became badly fogged. It was the scariest ride we had ever taken, but we all survived."

As Kerry and I approached the immigration station, I removed the radar detector from its mount on the windshield and stuffed it into the top of my tank bag.

"They'll find it if they search for it, but there's no point in advertising it," I thought as Kerry pulled to the side of the road, waved, and wished me well over the CB.

I pulled the motorcycle to the guard station and removed my helmet and earplugs.

I had ridden into Canada at least a half-dozen times before, entering at a different place each time. I have never made it into the country without a delay or an extensive search of the motorcycle. I hoped this time would be different.

"Where are you going?" the young man behind the drive-up window asked.

"To Hyder, Alaska," I replied.

"Why are you going to Hyder?"

"To meet my wife. She's waiting for me there so we can spend some vacation time together."

"What does your wife do in Hyder?"

"No, no. My wife lives in Texas with me, but has flown to Terrace and driven to Hyder to meet me so we can vacation in Alaska and Canada."

"Very well," the guard replied, as he filled out a small form, signed it, and passed it to me. "Take this form into the building over there and give it to someone behind the immigration desk. You can park your motorcycle right there." He motioned to a parking area adjacent to the building.

"Here we go again," I thought, as I placed my helmet on my head and steered the motorcycle to the immigration building. "I hope this doesn't require an hour and a half like it did at the Sweetgrass entry point a few years ago. That time I had to wait until the agents performed a background check, even after I exhibited evidence that I was registered to participate in the Alberta 2000 Endurance Rally in Edmonton.

When I entered the immigration station, I approached the only window that was staffed. The clerk was a very friendly, polite woman, about thirty years old.

"Hello. Welcome to Canada," she offered, with a big smile.

"Hello," I said as I offered her the form. "I'm on my way to Hyder, Alaska."

"Why do you want to go to Hyder," she asked.

I hesitated for a moment, then decided to tell her about my ride.

"I'll tell you what," I started. "I'm going to tell you the absolute truth. You may find it amusing or difficult to believe, but I'm going to be absolutely honest."

My approach was unexpected to her and set off some sort of warning signal. It was like she had been trained to be cautious when someone has a complicated explanation or reason for wanting to enter the country. The pleasant smile was replaced with uncertainty. Her eyes darted across the room to insure that several of the border guards were accessible. She had been leaning forward on the counter across the window from me, but she now stood upright, took a step back, and seemed to brace herself.

"I'm on a motorcycle that is parked right outside." I motioned toward the door. "A few hours ago, I broke the world record for visiting all of our 48 contiguous states by motorcycle. I started in Maine over six days ago. I'm trying to set a new record for visiting all 49 North American States in fewer than seven days. I've got to be in Hyder in about another sixteen hours in order to do it."

I waited for a reaction from the clerk. She continued to stare at me intensely. After a few moments, when she still hadn't responded, I continued.

"Look, all of my paperwork is on the motorcycle, so if you'll walk to the curb I'd be happy to show you my log book with all the signatures. I can also give you a copy of my route with the map and checkpoint locations."

The clerk let out a muffled giggle, held her hands to her mouth as if she had burped, then giggled uncontrollably.

"You're planning to ride a motorcycle from here to *Alaska* by tomorrow," she giggled. "That's impossible. Alaska is too far. It must be 3,000 kilometers from here."

"No, it's actually less than 900 miles to Hyder. That's the closest Alaskan town from here. It's on the peninsula of Alaska that extends way down south. It's only a few kilometers from Stewart."

"*Only* 900 miles? And you expect to make it on a motorcycle by tomorrow afternoon," she responded, between giggles. "Where are you staying tonight?"

"I'm not staying anywhere tonight. I'll have to ride straight through to make it in time." I began giggling with her. I began to feel like we were two drunks who just killed a bottle of whiskey. Anything we said seemed hilarious.

The thought flashed through my mind that perhaps the feat really was impossible. After all, how could I be certain I could make great time on the roads through the Canadian wilderness?

"Come with me," she directed, as she came from behind the counter and headed across the room toward the two guards. She continued giggling as she walked across the room, shook her head, and glanced back over her shoulder to be sure I was following. Now she seemed interested in amusing her friends.

"OK," she started, as we stopped in front of the guards. She hesitated for a moment as if to compose herself and say, "Let's make sure I've got this straight." She held her hands out, palms up as if stopping traffic, to emphasize that she was about to say something important. Then she let out another burst of giggles. I couldn't help but giggle along with her.

One guard smiled in anticipation of an interesting diversion. The other stared at me like a wooden Indian.

"This man is on a motorcycle," she continued. "*He* says he's just set some kind of world record for riding his motorcycle through all 48 states. Now he wants to go to Alaska and thinks he'll get there tomorrow afternoon." She paused to let out another giggle, then glanced at me as though she felt embarrassed for ridiculing me. "He wants to show us his motorcycle and forms and stuff to prove what he's doing. What do you guys think?"

"Great," the smiling guard remarked. His tone suggested, "sure, we'll play along with this for a while." He raised his body on the tips of his toes and craned his neck to look over us to see the motorcycle beyond the glass doors leading to the parking area. "What kind of motorcycle are you riding, a Harley?" he asked.

"No, it's a BMW," I responded. "You're welcome to take a look. I've got documentation to summarize the route I've taken and the places where I've stopped to validate my ride."

I glanced at the second guard, who appeared disinterested in the motorcycle, and whose eyes continued to study me. He wore a grim, sour look.

"Fine. Let's have a look at the motorcycle," Sourpuss mumbled, without any change to his expression. He led the way to the door with the three of us following closely behind.

When we reached the motorcycle, I opened the top case and extracted the binder with the witness forms. The guards seemed surprised at the cable securing the binder to the bike.

"I didn't want to lose this," I said as I unzipped the binder, turned to the forms for the state of Washington, and pointed to the signatures at the bottom of the page containing my photograph.

"These are the signatures that will validate my 48-state record." I turned a few pages to the divider that had been clearly labeled "Alaska." "This is the last set of forms I must have signed to establish the 49-state record. Here, let me give you guys a poop sheet on the ride," as I extended one of the sheets to each of the Canadians.

"And I suppose you're going to tell me you accomplished this without breaking any of the traffic laws of any of your 48 states?" Sourpuss snapped.

"Why of course," I responded with a wide smile. "I wouldn't have had it any other way."

"This is incredible. I can't believe this," Giggler marveled, no longer laughing. She studied the poop sheet intently.

"So what sort of gun do you carry?" Sourpuss asked.

"None. No guns, no knives, no weapons of any kind. Obviously, you're welcome to search the motorcycle. But I'm fully aware of the laws here in Canada. You won't find anything improper."

The two guards looked at each other for a moment. I was quite certain that a search of the motorcycle would ensue, particularly if Sourpuss had his way. "The motorcycle world is waiting for me, and I'm possibly going to be screwed-up by some stupid, petty bureaucrat," I thought.

"Just go ahead," the other guard remarked. "Be careful of the wildlife up here, and good luck. I hope you make the record."

"Yes. *Please* be careful," Giggler implored, as she folded the poop sheet and held it close to her breast, something she now apparently cherished. She wasn't giggling anymore. She had reverted back to the sincere, helpful clerk whom I had encountered during my first 30 seconds with her.

Sourpuss looked on, with no change in his expression or demeanor.

"Doesn't this boy ever smile?" I thought and almost asked. I resisted the urge to have some fun, however. "Probably the wrong time to be a smart-ass," I reasoned.

As I pulled away from the immigration station, I decided to stop to study the route from here to Hyder, and calculate *exactly* how much time I could afford to nap. At about this time, Michael Gasper was posting a message to LDRIDER from his home in Seattle. Excerpts from Michael's message reflected my condition very well:

> *Unfortunately, yesterday was the worst day of riding in Ron's personal riding career. That is according to his own words. He ran into a hell of a storm, and he ran out of gas in extreme rural Nevada. That cost him valuable sleep time, and he was showing it today.*

> *. . . At this moment, he has 900 miles left to go for the entire trip to Hyder, Alaska, and about 17 hours to do it. But consider this: he is very tired, sore, exhausted, and the roads in far northern Canada are not that great for making time. He still has a long road to ride, and the worst road conditions.*

I stopped at a McDonalds restaurant in Abbotsford, a small town a few miles north of the border. This would be the first time since leaving Maine more than six days ago that I would sit down at a table to eat. I ordered my meal and spread my maps on the table. For the first time, I studied the route to Hyder closely to determine how much slack there really was in my schedule. Because I had always regarded this portion of the trip as a whimsical afterthought, I hadn't planned it as thoroughly as I had the rest of the trip.

"Just beat the 48-state record, then make a mad dash for Hyder," had been my attitude. "Try to get to Hyder in less than a week, but what the hell if you can't? No one has ever documented a 49-state ride anyway, so it's not like there is already a 49-state record to be broken."

When I prepared my route sheets, I had planned to take the shortest route from Sumas to Hyder. I was going to use Route 1 from the Canadian border to Cache Creek, following the Frazer River through Falls Creek and Spences Bridge. From Cache Creek, I would take Route 97 to Prince George, then Route 16 to Kitwanga and the Cassier Highway to Hyder.

The first thing I noticed was that if I rode from here to Hyder at the legal speed limit, I would have no time for sleep. I had nearly 900 miles to Hyder and only 15 hours for the ride, if I was going to do the 49-states in seven days or less. It had been 16 hours since I woke from my three hours of sleep in Utah. After all I had just done, I didn't expect to wrap it up with 30 hours of continuous riding.

I decided to ride at a very brisk pace and put time "in the bank" before I stopped for sleep.

The route I had planned to Cache Creek was a very thin, squiggly line through the Lillooet Range of the Coast Mountains. I tried to imagine what the road might be like and shuddered at the thought of having to drive it in my exhausted state, between midnight and 3:00 a.m. Visions of a narrow, winding mountain road infested with moose, elk, bear, and deer filled my imagination. And I knew it would be getting cold.

It's one thing to face the possibility of striking deer on such roads at night. I've faced that risk often in the United States.

It's quite another to know that if you strike one in the Canadian wilderness and are injured or disabled, you face the additional danger of becoming a bear's next meal. It gives a new meaning to the term "Meals on Wheels."

A few miles to the east there was a much thicker, straight line representing the Coquihalla Highway, a toll road leading to Merritt and continuing to Route 1 near Kamloops. By riding farther, I could take a presumably less tiring, safer route to Kamloops, then take Route 1 west to Cache Creek and continue as originally planned. It appeared the easier ride would add no more than 75 miles to my trip. I hoped the faster speed I would be able to maintain on the less stressful route would compensate for the additional distance.

As I folded my map and prepared to leave the restaurant, I began to plan for the sleep I would require before reaching Hyder. The best strategy would be to postpone a nap long enough so that I would awaken just as the sun was rising. If I succumbed too early, and had to continue riding again before sunrise, I would be very drowsy and might very well have to nap again, as I had in Colorado. If I could last until shortly before daybreak, I would benefit from the significant natural alertness in alertness that accompanies the sunrise. Fortunately, being this far north, I knew it would begin getting light very early at this time of year.

After entering the toll road, I was convinced I had made the correct choice of routes to Cache Creek. I was certain the more direct route couldn't be as good a route as the first-class Coquihalla Highway. I complimented myself for being smart enough to make such a wise choice in spite of my exhausted state. I also realized that after leaving the highway in Kamloops, the remaining 750 miles to Hyder would be on secondary, two-lane roads.

I became very cold on the way to Kamloops, but resisted the temptation to stop and put on additional clothing. I knew I would have to temporarily become colder while I removed my riding suit, shirt, and pants to start the layering from the bottom, beginning with long underwear. I also knew the warmth and comfort could make me sleepier. Despite this, I finally decided it would be more risky to continue to ride while cold. Even with a temperature of 40 degrees, I knew that traveling faster than 60 mph would provide a wind chill well below zero.

I stopped west of Kamloops, parked the motorcycle, stripped down, and dressed again, beginning with my long underwear. I was very cold but knew this would be the last time I would go through the process. The road was very desolate and not a single vehicle passed to challenge my modesty.

Upon leaving Cache Creek and the Coastal Mountains, the terrain changed. As I entered the Fraser Plateau beyond Cache Creek, the forest grew thicker, but the road was straight and presented few challenges. I soon became drowsy and decided to nap at the first opportunity. Near Chasm, I discovered a small rest area with concrete picnic tables and benches. I set the Screaming Meanie for 90 minutes and laid down on one of the concrete benches, after placing a pair of gloves under my helmet. As I prepared to lay down, I became concerned about sleeping for 8 hours and killing any chance I had of achieving my goal. I feared the battery in the Screaming Meanie would run down or that the inexpensive device would otherwise malfunction. I felt stupid for not having two Screaming Meanies and vowed never to let that happen again.

I hadn't intended to sleep beside the road in Canada or Alaska. As I was planning the trip, I expected to stop for a few hours at a motel between Washington and Hyder. But unlike the United States portion of the trip, I hadn't made any motel reservations in Canada.

My fear of encountering brown bears, particularly the Grizzlies found throughout British Columbia, made me reluctant to stop beside the road in Canada. As I lay on the bench, I thought briefly about the possibility of being awakened by a hungry carnivore. I hoped that my helmet and riding suit would offer me enough protection to wake up and then activate the Screaming Meanie. Surely that would drive any beast away.

Despite my fears, I fell asleep immediately and was awakened 90 minutes later by the Screaming Meanie. I felt very stiff as I attempted to rise from the bench, chalked it up to age, and limped toward my motorcycle. As tired as I was, when I approached the motorcycle, I was struck by the sheer beauty of the vehicle. It reminded me of the excitement I often feel when I walk into my garage after not having ridden for a while. At such times, I wonder how I can love the sight of a machine so much. And then I remember that it's not just the machine, but the notion of adventure and excitement the vehicle invokes.

It was just beginning to become light. Although stiff, I felt mentally refreshed and committed to continue riding until I reached Hyder.

I refueled in Williams Lake and again in Prince George. While I was refueling in Prince George, Barbara, Tracy, Chris, and Herb were entering the café at the King Edward Hotel in Stewart to have breakfast, where they group encountered Vince Kretzul, president of Black Gold Beemers in Edmonton, who had also come to Hyder to help celebrate the conclusion of my ride. The group learned that only the previous evening Vince had experienced precisely the type of tragedy I had feared; seventy-five miles from Hyder, Vince had demolished his motorcycle when he'd struck a moose. He accompanied his motorcycle down a steep, rocky ravine. Although badly bruised, Vince fared much better than the moose. After making it's way down the ravine on the opposite side of the road, the moose lay down to die. Vince could hear the baying of the dying animal from his side of the road and worried that the distress call would attract bears.

To attract the attention of motorists who happened by, Vince tossed luggage and parts of the motorcycle up the hill and into the roadway. The litter attracted the attention of some truck drivers, who helped extricate Vince from the ravine and gave him a ride into Stewart, where he checked into the King Edward. Vince was looking for someone who could drive him into Hyder when he came upon his group of friends having breakfast at the café.

When the group returned to Hyder, they noticed a new sign that had been placed over a small gift shop, Northern Stars, anticipating my arrival in Hyder. "Way to Go Ronnie," the sign read. Barbara had met the owners of the shop when she arrived in Hyder the previous day. Mike and Suzi Craft had moved to Hyder several years ago from McKinney, Texas, which is only

Suzi Craft displays her support for Ron at Northern Stars Gift Shop in Hyder.

about 15 miles from our home in Plano. After their conversation, the Crafts checked out my web site to learn more about my ride.

Barbara also discovered that large congratulatory signs had been placed on the door to our room at the Sealaska Inn and over the hotel's bar. As word of my impending arrival spread through the small town, additional signs of congratulations appeared.

LDRIDER was jammed with activity. As I was approaching Burns Lake, Bill Koehler was posting a message to the list:

I have been reading this mail list for a few months now. This, in addition to the Iron Butt web site as well as various other web sites, has changed me into a long-distance rider "will-be" (as compared to a wannabe). However, the real clincher was witnessing for Ron in Pennsylvania.

In addition, following the list very closely over the past week to check on Ron's progress has shown me what a

*great bunch of people there are here. I have never
experienced a group of people spread out over the
country that are so close to one another.*

*I presently ride a Bandit 1200 and am looking to get
either a BMW or ST1100 later this year. For now, I am
planning my first SaddleSore 1000 in the next few
weeks as my personal initiation.*

*I apologize for rambling on like this when I know
everyone is on the edge of their seat waiting for word
from Hyder (like I am).*

Bill Koehler

When I stopped to refuel in Burns Lake, a motorist approached and appeared interested in the motorcycle. After admiring the motorcycle, he asked where I was headed.

"I'm on my way to Hyder, Alaska," I answered.

"Ahh, yes, Hyder. Let's see now. That's about seven more hours."

"No, it's only about five," I shot back. I'm sure my voice held a tone of desperation because he took a step back and looked at me strangely, obviously startled by my emphatic reply.

"Have you made the trip before?" he asked softly.

I felt silly for declaring that the ride would require less than five hours simply because that was all the time I had available.

"Well, no. But I've studied the map pretty good and I think I can make it in five hours if I keep moving."

"Well the map may be a little confusing," the stranger continued. "I've made the trip a lot. The road actually goes north of Hyder to the Meziadin Junction to get around the Cambria Icefield," he continued, as his finger traced an arc in the air to represent the route to Hyder.

"Thanks a lot for the information," I responded, as I prepared to leave. "I'll just have to do the best I can and see how it turns out." Actually, I now had only about four and a half hours to make what this Canadian felt was a seven-hour trip.

As I pulled away from the filling station I chuckled to myself, reflecting on how arrogant I must have appeared for arguing about something I didn't know. "No wonder there's that slur about the 'Ugly American,' " I thought.

Even in my exhausted state, riding through the Canadian wilderness was beautiful and I tried to enjoy it. A short way beyond Burns Lake, the route got more mountainous again as Route 16 wended its way into the Hazleton Mountains. Several times during this part of the ride I remembered reading that Hyder is halfway between New York and Tokyo. There was something I liked about that notion. It seemed poetic, somehow.

Back in Hyder, the welcoming party had grown to include Rick Morrison and Norm and Linda Babcock. Not sure when I'd arrive, Herb, Tracy, Don, and Chris left Hyder about 11:30 a.m. to meet me on the road and to escort me to Hyder. The rest of the group gathered in the former town museum, which Caroline had opened for them. It provided an excellent vantage point, being only about a half a block from the border.

After a while, Barbara called Roberta and learned that Herb had just called for a status report as they waited to intercept me. Herb's call, one of the last calls placed to my toll-free number during my seven-day ride, was the 150th call received during the week.

Knowing that my arrival was not imminent, the group dispersed around town.

Rick went with the Babcocks to the bar at the Sealaska Inn, and visited with Gary Benedict, the owner. Rick received several phone calls while waiting for me, including one from Mike Gasper. Rick promised to call Mike as soon as I arrived. Eventually, Barbara joined them. "Aren't you chewing your fingernails off, waiting for him? Why don't you use my CB to see if you can raise him or the guys who are out there waiting for him," Gary offered. She tried the CB but was unsuccessful.

I continued to Kitwanga, where I made my last fuel stop on the way to Hyder. There is a large "North to Alaska" sign at the intersection of Routes 16 and 37:

Stewart	237 km
Hyder, Alaska	240 km
Bear Glacier	201 km

I looked at the clock and performed a quick calculation. I still had to ride more than 140 miles. To accomplish the ride in less than 7 days, I would have to cover the remaining distance in about an hour and 45 minutes. That worked out to an *average* speed of about 82 mph.

Averaging 82 mph for that long on secondary roads through wildlife-infested mountains and forests, after having come the last 1,700 miles on only 90 minutes of sleep, seemed hopeless. But after all I had done to come this far, I wanted to make it to Hyder in time to establish the record I had been seeking. I twisted the throttle wide open and blasted across the Skeena River.

I recalled an e-mail message from Jerry Clemmons from North Carolina, describing what I should expect on this final stretch of highway. Jerry, a finisher of the Iron Butt Rally in 1995 and 1997, had been to Hyder twice before. In his message Jerry wrote:

> *I've never seen a moose on the road, however, there are warning signs every few miles. I've never seen a Bear on the Cassier, either. I think they're all in Hyder, eating the world's largest, fresh Chum Salmon out of the streams. They are known to roam the streets at night, occasionally wandering into one of the bars.*

In the same message, Jerry also reminded me of an experience I had been looking forward to:

> *Don't forget to get Hyderized at the Glacier Inn, or Eternity Bar, as it's called now since the filming of the movie 'Leaving Normal'. I didn't do that on my first trip up there and had to go back a second time. They give you two shot glasses. One is a double-shot of Everclear, the other is water for a chaser. You have to swig down the Everclear in one throw. They then turn the glass upside down on the bar top, light the remains with a cigarette lighter, and with the bar in flames, proclaim you have just been Hyderized. You get a written certificate of this. Mine is at our store, under the glass on my desk with a bunch of other memorabilia.*

The Everclear closes your throat and makes you talk in a whisper for a couple of minutes. Conversation stops, as does the pool game. All eyes are on you as the local patrons cross their fingers in hopes that you'll throw up. But hold it down. Otherwise, according to tradition, you have to buy everyone in the house a round.

As the excitement continued to grow, Michael Gasper posted another message:

I just spoke with Rick Morrison on the phone two seconds ago.

Rick . . . is waiting in Hyder.

Don Moses is 10 miles up the road, waiting for Ron, to escort him into Hyder.

Herb Anderson is 60 miles up the road, waiting for Ron, to escort him into Hyder.

Barb is getting anxious, and concerned.

Tension is in the air . . . in Hyder.

Nerves are breaking . . . all over America.

Rick Morrison and Barbara wait for Ron in Hyder, Alaska.

Rick will call me the second that Ron appears in
Hyder.

Michael

Thom Irwin responded to Michael's message with his own
post to the list:

I have been truly amazed by this whole project. If there
is any time left for public rooting for Ron's success I'm
doing it now.

Go Ron, go!

Thom Irwin

I held the accelerator open and watched my speed climb. I
hadn't seen any RCMP patrol cars since entering Canada the
previous evening. As I reached the crest of a hill and began
down the other side, an RCMP was writing a ticket to a vehicle
that had been pulled to the side of the road. I eased off the throttle.

"This is a sign that I'm going to make it," I thought. *Yes,* I
shouted, as I passed the patrol car. "There can't be more than
one or two of these guys in this part of the world, and I've just
had the good fortune to come across him while he's busy with a
customer. I'm going to make it after all." I cranked the throttle
wide open again.

With about 75 miles to go, I saw a rider approaching from
the opposite direction. As we passed and exchanged waves, I
recognized Chris Baldwin on his red Honda ST1100. I didn't
slow down, but glanced at my rear-view mirror. I could see
Chris making a U-turn to follow me. Chris was on a tight schedule and had headed for home when I didn't arrive in Hyder as
expected.

Within a few minutes, three more riders approached. As we
passed, I recognized Herb, Tracy, and Don. These three riders
also executed U-turns and began following Chris and me.

I didn't want to slow down for a discussion, but I hoped one
of them would take the lead for the rest of the trip. Herb Anderson wondered if I wanted him to do so, as he pulled beside me,

and I extended my open hand to the road ahead, welcoming him to take the lead. I knew Herb could set a very brisk pace.

Herb is an experienced rider who usually serves as "Road Captain" for long rides sponsored by Black Gold Beemers in Edmonton. When Herb's children, Erik and Nikolette were young, Herb and his wife Ruth sold their home, packed their motorcycles, and left for a ten-month family vacation through Canada, the United States, and Mexico. I've always admired people like Herb and Ruth, whose personal mantra is "follow your dreams." The courage required to do as the Anderson's have done is rare, even in the riding community.

As we approached Stewart, we slowed to cross a long, wooden bridge. Wood bridges are notorious for being slippery when wet and I was careful not to screw up the ride by dropping my motorcycle this close to the finish.

Caroline was on the phone with the gasoline station in Stewart as we passed, now little more than a mile from the border. Caroline had called the station to ask the attendant to be on the lookout for us.

"How many are you looking for?" the attendant asked. "I just saw five fly by here like bats out of hell."

Caroline thanked the attendant, jumped into her truck, and raced for the Sealaska Inn to alert the group. Barbara was already walking toward the border when Caroline zoomed up in the truck, told her about my imminent arrival, and continued on to the Sealaska Inn to alert Rick and the Babcocks.

Don Moses had been trying to raise me on the CB ever since joining up with me, but my radio had been turned off since shortly after entering Canada. As we approached Hyder, I remembered that Don's motorcycle was equipped with a CB, so I turned mine on again.

"Sorry, Don. I've just put my ears on again," I remarked over the CB.

Hyder, Alaska
Approaching the border crossing, there is a small Canadian Customs office on the left side of the road. A few hundred feet beyond, where the pavement ends, a large "Welcome to Hyder,

Alaska" sign is suspended across the road. The posted speed limit is 20 mph. I was pleased to find there was no United States Customs Office, so I wasn't delayed entering the United States.

As we approached the border, Herb pulled to the shoulder to permit me to lead the way. As we passed beneath the sign, my companions began blowing their horns in celebration.

As I was extending my side stand to prepare to stop, Don's voice cracked over the CB.

"Well Ron, I hope it was later than 6:27 p.m. when you left Kittery. The official satellite time shown on my GPS says 6:27 p.m. Eastern time right now."

"Thanks Don," I responded. "I think I've made it under the seven-day goal by a few minutes."

I looked up the unpaved street toward the small town and saw Barbara hurrying in my direction, followed by Rick Morrison, Norm, and Linda.

Caroline Gutierrez welcomes Ron to Hyder, along with Norm Babcock, Herb Anderson, Chris Baldwin, and Don Moses.

Vince Kretzul, Ron, Chris Baldwin, Tracy DesLaurier, Herb
Anderson, Don Moses, Norm Babcock, Rick Morrison, and Caroline
Gutierrez celebrate after Ron's arrival in Hyder (photo by Barbara
Robinson).

Seeing my good friend Rick was a total surprise, as he had-
n't told anyone he would be in Hyder. He delayed his decision
until he was sure we would have something to celebrate. Rick
and I had participated in a lot of rallies together and he won the
1997 Iron Butt Rally.

I prepared for the signing ritual for the final time. As I unzipped the cover of the binder and removed Dale's pen from my
breast pocket, I chuckled to myself again about the rotation of
writing instruments that had taken place during the past week.

After Tracy, Chris, Herb, Vince, and Don signed my witness
forms, I asked Caroline Gutierrez, my official Hyder resident
witness, to sign the last witness form in the binder, signifying
the completion of my 49-state journey.

Day	State	Miles Ridden	Miles to Go
7	49	8,798	0

During the last seven days, I had stopped for fuel 90 times.
Except for the meal at McDonalds shortly after I crossed into
Canada, all other food that I had during the week was con-

Ron and Barbara prepare to ride back from the border to the
Sealaska Inn in Hyder (photo by Linda Babcock).

Linda Babcock, Ron, Herb Anderson (background), Tracy
DesLaurier, and Chris Baldwin congratulate Ron for completing the
ride to Hyder.

Rons' welcome sign is prominent on the Glacier Inn Bar (photo by
Barbara Robinson).

sumed while I was standing at a gasoline pump. I averaged 52.4
mph during the week (58.9 hours while awake) and slept a little
over eighteen hours. Fourteen hours of that sleep was divided
across four motel stops. The remaining four hours were divided
across three "Iron Butt Motel" stops. I made it through the entire trip without a single cup of coffee and without taking any
aspirin or other pills.

After getting my forms signed and taking several photographs to commemorate the event, Barbara showed me to our
room at the hotel. Although tired, I was also hungry. After
cleaning up, we went to the bar for a few beers, then had an
early dinner with the group. During dinner, Suzi Craft of
Northern Stars came to the table and presented me with a commemorative photo of Hyder with a congratulatory message.
The photograph was taken at the border where I had crossed,
with the "Welcome to Hyder" sign clearly visible. There were
two bears crossing the road beneath the sign.

During dinner, I was summoned to the phone several times
to receive congratulatory phone calls from Mike Pecora, Jerry
Clemmons, and Michael Gasper.

Ron, Tracy DesLaurier, Don Moses, Vince Kretzul, Herb Anderson, and Rick Morrison celebrate at the Sealaska Inn in Hyder.

Rick Morrison presented me with a box of fine cigars he had obtained while in Argentina recently. He knew that I occasionally enjoyed a fine cigar, because the last time Rick was our houseguest, we shared some Cuban Cohibas I had obtained while in Madrid.

After dinner, Barbara and I returned to the room for a five-hour nap. We set our alarm for 11:00 p.m. because Rick, Tracy, Herb, Vince, Norm, Barbara, and I wanted to get "Hyderized."

Steve Wilson was posting a message that reflected the attitude of many of the riders who had been following my ride:

Thank God! I haven't left this computer for the last 4 hours. Now I can go drain the bladder and breathe a sigh of relief.

Congratulations Ron !!!!!!!!!!

I have now met a bona fide "Hero."

Steve Wilson

After returning to Vancouver, Chris Baldwin posted a message to the LDRIDER list describing the last hour of my ride:

I just got home from Vancouver, BC, after witnessing Ron's arrival in Hyder yesterday. Four of us—Herb

*Anderson, Tracy DesLaurier, Don Moses, and I—rode
with him for the last 129 km of his feat. He rode up to
180 k/hr in the straightaways and hard through the
curves. The road is a narrow two-lane with lots of hills
and twists and moose and bear and it was raining
hard. The few cars and RVs on the road saw nothing
but a yellow (Herb), gray (Ron), blue (Tracy), red (me)
and black (Don) blur as we went by. Afterward, Herb
Anderson caught the enormity of what Ron had done
when he said that our experience as witnesses would
be like being on the top of Mt. Everest when Hillary
reached the pinnacle. And Ron himself was very
generous in allowing all of us to be part of what he
had done, not just spectators. Wow!*

Chris Baldwin

Soon after the message was posted, Joe Zulaski posted a response to Chris' message:

*Man, I know what you mean. I felt like a part of
history the whole time I was riding with him in
Washington State. It was one of those times that you
tell yourself, "you gotta remember this for the rest of
your life 'cuz it's so special!"*

*That's why I felt he was a true gentleman. He was big
enough to share this event with soooo many people.
How many of us would have done the same so
unselfishly? I mean, it could have cost him the record.
However, in every report I read, he was so courteous
and thoughtful to bystanders and witnesses, that he
must have spent many extra minutes at each stop just
to express his thanks and gratitude to these (us) people
for showing up.*

*Ron, I can't say it enough. "You're a class act." Barb,
you know how to pick 'em!*

Joe Zulaski

Although many people thanked me for letting them share
in the event, I was the true beneficiary of their participation.
Perhaps the greatest compliment of all was offered by the rider
whose record I broke, Mike Kneebone. In an article by Jeff
Dean, Mike was quoted as saying:

Barbara and Ron relax at Hyder, Alaska.

I can't think of a more exciting time for the long-distance community. In any given year, one or two riders had tried to break the record, but none had even come close. When Ron first mentioned he was looking at the ride, I knew he'd be the one to topple the record someday. Ron spent years planning and researching the challenge and then he went out and made crushing our record look easy. Adding the Alaska leg was nothing short of brilliant. There is little doubt that both of Ron's records, 48 states in 6 days and 49 states in 7 days will be on the record books for a long, long time. But most of all, I can't think of a more deserving person to hold these records than Ron Ayres!

Monday morning several of us revisited the site of Vince's accident to help him retrieve his motorcycle. As we approached the location where Vince had killed the moose, we met a wrecker that was retrieving a pickup truck from the scene of another accident. The driver followed us to the scene of Vince's accident to help us drag Vince's demolished motorcycle from the ravine. I used the opportunity to take some photos of Vince and the moose, or what remained of it. In the eighteen hours since the moose was killed, wild animals had eaten much of the hind-quarter. I presented one of the antlers to Vince as a souvenir.

Before we helped Vince retrieve his demolished motorcycle from the ravine, I asked the Babcocks, Rick, Tracy, and Herb to

Vince Kretzul and Ron examine the damage to the moose road kill
(after the animals had a crack at it).

Vince Kretzul stands in the ravine with his wrecked motorcycle.

arrange the motorcycles under the "Welcome to Hyder" sign at the border for a commemorative photograph. At the last moment, I asked Vince to get into the picture, even though his motorcycle had been demolished in the accident with the moose. Vince stood beside us with his helmet under his arm.

The photograph was taken at the same spot as the photograph of the bears that Suzi Craft had presented to me at dinner on Sunday night. It's one of my favorites and I included it on my web site. I had an enlargement made for each of the riders in the photograph. Unfortunately, Chris and Don had left Hyder before the shot was taken.

When Don saw the photograph on my web site, I received an e-mail message expressing his regret for not having waited to be included in the photograph.

"You will either understand totally, or think me an empty-minded fool, but I mark missing lining my bike up for that picture in Hyder as one of the great tragedies of my life," Don wrote.

I assured Don that I understood totally.

Norm Babcock, Linda Babcock, Ron, Tracy DesLaurier, Rick Morrison, Herb Anderson, and Vince Kretzul commemorate the occasion with a group photograph (photo by Barbara Robinson).

11

Alaska to Edmonton

Although I felt rested enough to depart for Edmonton, where I would participate in the Alberta 2000 Rally, I liked the idea of spending a relaxing day in Hyder, so Barbara and I delayed our departure until Tuesday morning.

Before the trip I had attempted to buy Barbara a First Gear Solo Expedition riding suit like the one I obtained for the 49-state ride. Since the standard sizes wouldn't fit her, I presented her with a custom-made Aerostich. I'm not usually fashion conscious about riding equipment, but I liked the idea of wearing matching suits, so Barbara brought my Aerostich to Hyder. I shipped my First Gear suit, the water jug that had occupied the passenger seat, and my receipts and witness forms back to Texas.

We stopped at the King Edward Hotel in Stewart for breakfast. As we were preparing to leave, a passerby stopped, expressed interest in our trip, and admired the motorcycle. He wished us well as we departed.

Several hours later, as we were about 35 miles from Smithers, I noticed my temperature gauge rise into the danger zone. I slowed the motorcycle and pulled onto the shoulder. No sooner had I stopped than an SUV pulled in behind me. The man who we had spoken to us outside the King Edward Hotel emerged from the vehicle.

"Your motorcycle deposited a whole lot of something on the road a few miles back," the man said. "I don't know if it was oil or antifreeze or what, but there sure was a lot of it ejected from the bike."

I examined the sight gauge and confirmed that I had lost a significant amount of coolant from the radiator.

"Is there anything I can do to help?" the man asked. "I have plenty of tools if you need them."

"Thanks, but I don't think I'm prepared to make any roadside repairs," I answered. "How far am I from civilization? I've got a cellular phone. Perhaps I can contact a towing service."

"The next major town is Smithers. I don't know exactly how far away we are though."

The man's wife poked her head from the vehicle, as if she had anticipated my thoughts, and already tried her cellular phone. "We're too far out to be able to place a call," she announced.

"If you want to try to make it to the next town, I'd be happy to follow behind you," the man offered.

"Thanks, I'd appreciate it."

By the time we continued, the temperature gauge had fallen into the safe zone. But the needle soon moved back into the danger zone and I pulled to the shoulder again. The couple in the SUV once again stopped with me.

"I appreciate your helpfulness, but I suggest you go on," I remarked as the man approached the motorcycle again. "I'm going to have to continue to stop when the temperature rises. It may take a while to reach the next town this way, but I've got plenty of daylight left to do it."

"Are you sure?" the man asked. "I don't mind staying with you."

I assured him there wasn't anything he could do, so he continued on. He was plainly reluctant to leave us stranded.

And so it went for the next few hours. On the few occasions when there was a downhill run, I'd switch the engine off and coast to allow the wind to cool the inactive engine. Whenever the temperature rose into the danger zone, we would stop again. After some time we encountered a sign noting the distance to Smithers. When we were within a few miles of town, and once again had to stop to permit the engine to cool, I tried the cellular phone again. I was now able to get a signal and called my mechanic, George Mitmanski, at BMW of North Dallas.

I explained the situation and asked him how to refill the radiator with coolant.

"It's not an easy process, Ron. You have to remove the fuel tank in order to get to the filler. I think you need to try to find a motorcycle dealer to help you with this problem."

George obviously knew of my mechanical limitations.

"Don't drive the motorcycle with the temperature gauge in the danger zone or it will damage the engine," George concluded.

We continued to Smithers. As we entered the town, Barbara flipped her face shield open, tapped me on the shoulder, and shouted that I had just passed a Harley-Davidson dealership. I executed a U-turn and returned to the dealer.

Although the shop only sold Harley-Davidsons, the mechanic, David Clement, offered to help. It didn't take long for him to discover that a radiator hose was disconnected, permitting the coolant to leak. Figuring out how to remove the fairing to gain access to the hose and then replace the fluid took a while. The shop was about to close, but David willingly worked beyond closing time to repair the motorcycle. In the meantime, Barbara scouted local motels. Although we had intended to get much farther, the notion of calling it quits early and having a nice dinner and a few beers was too appealing to resist. We took a room in a motel adjacent to the motorcycle dealer and continued our journey the next morning.

We arrived in Jasper late the next afternoon and checked into a nice log cabin. It had been more than a week since I had been on the computer, so I walked to the registration area to see if I could use a phone line to get connected. I had nearly 1,000 messages backlogged. This included several hundred general messages from LDRIDER, but there were hundreds more that were specifically about my recent adventure. I spent several hours going through them, answering some, and saving others for later.

One of my favorites was from Jim Hickerson. I was very humbled as I read:

Congratulations Ron and family,

The world wants its sports heroes to be worthy of the term. Too often it gets a snotty tennis player or a drug-addicted major leaguer who takes the money and says "to hell with the rest of you, I have my own life to live." This time, for seven grueling days we got more than we deserve. The achievement speaks for itself. Meanwhile, the Internet messages from checkpoint observers tell a remarkably similar story of grit, patience, humor, thoughtfulness, determination, and human kindness. I witnessed it briefly myself.

Thanks, Ron, for being the kind of motorcyclist that makes us all look better: A rider's rider and a gentleman. A worthy world record-holder. Today we all share in your triumph.

Jim Hickerson

On Thursday morning we continued to Edmonton. As we approached the city, I took a small secondary road south in an effort to avoid city traffic. When we were about 45 miles from Edmonton, a deer suddenly appeared directly in front of the motorcycle. We didn't see it until it was directly in front of us, as it was running at full speed across the road from heavy brush. There was no time to brake or to swerve to avoid hitting it. We were traveling about 60 mph when the impact occurred.

We expected the motorcycle to go down. My first thought after the impact was, "Is Barbara still on the bike?"

As the bike wobbled and began to lose stability, a conversation that I had with Steve Losofsky a few months before flashed through my mind.

The original owner of Reno BMW, Steve was an experienced flat-track racer and an expert rider. While on his way back to Nevada from a trip to Daytona Bike Week, Steve was our house guest. He told us that while riding to Texas in a construction zone in heavy rain, his motorcycle slipped into a rut caused by two adjacent uneven lanes. His motorcycle began to shimmy and he worried about losing control.

"Reverting to my old racing days, I gave the bike full throttle," Steve related. "I remembered that in a lot of situations, blasting through with maximum acceleration is better than slowing down."

When I hit the deer, the conversation flashed into my mind immediately. I remembered Steve standing at our kitchen counter, laughing and motioning with an exaggerated twist of his wrist and upper torso to emphasize how he managed to regain control of his motorcycle.

I cranked the accelerator fully open. After a moment, the bike stabilized and I slowed down and pulled to the side of the road. "Thank you, Steve Losofsky," I thought. "Thank you very much."

I brought the motorcycle to a stop about a tenth of a mile from the point of impact. "Oh the poor deer," Barbara lamented. "Do you think we killed it? What if it's just injured and suffering?"

I couldn't help but ask, "Do you have any idea just how lucky we are?"

We walked down the road and found the deer dead. It was clear the impact killed the animal instantly.

The bike came through with surprisingly little damage. The radiator was obviously damaged, as the coolant was once again running on the road. The fairing was cracked in several places and had apparently buckled loose from its mounts. The front fender was also cracked and a small piece of fur was embedded in the cracks.

I rode the bike to the motel, driving slowly to avoid subjecting the damaged parts to additional stress. The coolant continued to leak all the way to the hotel, but the engine didn't overheat.

Needless to say, Barbara and I felt very, very fortunate. Not only did we reflect on the personal injury we could have suffered, but either of the incidents of the last several days, had they occurred during the previous week, would have ended my hope of setting the new records.

Mike Kneebone's message summarized the situation very well:

Ron,

*You might think hitting a deer is bad luck, and I
suppose it is. But given what happened, you are the
luckiest two people on the face of the earth!*

Face it Ron, June, 1998 is Ron Ayres month!

I am sincerely glad to hear you are OK!

Michael Kneebone

I made arrangements for the motorcycle to be repaired,
then flew back to Texas with Barbara.

I've never been convinced one way or the other about the ef-
fectiveness of deer whistles. But the only time I've struck a deer
is also the only time I've ridden without them. I had intended to
place a set of whistles of the type Jan Cutler at Reno BMW ad-
vocates, but hadn't gotten around to it before the ride. I don't intend to ride without them again.

My friends and coworkers have always been supportive and
enthusiastic about my participation in endurance rides. My ad-
ministrative assistant, Marcie Leist, had followed my progress
on the Internet and insured that others in the company were
apprized of my progress.

When I returned to work, I found my office decorated extensively in celebration of my accomplishment. A life-size deer
mannequin stood in the corner. A two-gallon gas can with red,
white, and blue streamers extending from the spout was on my
desk. Banners were strung from one corner of the ceiling to the
other. A fresh bunch of bananas had been placed in a fruit bowl
on my credenza and toy motorcycles were arranged on my book-
case.

Later, I was summoned to a meeting in one of our conference rooms. When I opened the door I was surprised by a group
of employees assembled around a large cake that had been decorated with a banana. I was presented with a compass, to insure I wouldn't become lost again. I was awarded a small
trophy. I was also given a bottle of "Middle Age Crazy Pills,"
guaranteed to help me act my age.

12

Riding Home

I wasn't able to participate in the Alberta 2000 because of the damage caused to my motorcycle by the deer strike, but I delivered a brief talk about the 49-state ride.

I returned to Edmonton to retrieve the repaired *KLONE* on Thursday evening, July 2, intending to use the long July 4th weekend to ride back to Texas.

The direct route home would avoid the mountains and include riding through Alberta, Saskatchewan, the Dakotas, Nebraska, Kansas, and Oklahoma. This route was less than 2,000 miles, but I didn't want to sacrifice a holiday weekend on such a boring route. Instead, I selected a 2,400-mile route that included a side trip through the Grand Tetons of Wyoming and the Colorado Rockies. I planned to use the trip as an opportunity to work on a new project.

A few weeks earlier Dan Kennedy at Whitehorse Press sent me a book, *World Motorcycle Endurance Racing,* by Mark Wernham and Mick Walker. The book contained hundreds of high-quality color photographs from the Bol d'Or, which dominates the Endurance Racing scene, and other major races. Dan suggested that I consider a long-term project to collect quality photographs relating to endurance *riding* (as opposed to endurance *racing*) and develop a book with a similar format. I arranged to meet Randell Hendricks, who had been a witness in Texas, in Buena Vista, Colorado, to help set up some shots in the mountains.

There was nothing spectacular about the route south to Calgary and Fort Macleod. The ride became interesting only after passing into the United States when Route 89 approached the Lewis Range at the Glacier National Park.

It started to rain while I was still in Canada and continued to get heavier as I moved south. I was starting to feel a little chilly and put on my heated vest at my last fuel stop in Canada.

The Storm

I arrived in Choteau, Montana, at about 7:30 p.m. and picked up Route 287 to Augusta. I could see heavy, dark storm clouds to the southwest. I knew that storms usually move in from the west, and hoped I could make it beyond the storm's path.

When I reached Augusta, the rain was heavier and the wind had increased. The black skies to the southwest looked ominous. I considered waiting in Augusta until the weather cleared, but I was already running late and was concerned about making Buena Vista in time for my meeting with Randell. I continued to ride.

After leaving Augusta, the rain intensified, the wind became more violent, and lightning struck nearby, illuminating the surrounding area. The wind was so powerful that it was difficult to keep the motorcycle upright. It began to hail. I knew that tornadoes are often preceded by violent summer hailstorms. Water was becoming deep on the road. I stopped the motorcycle and executed a U-turn, intending to return to Augusta to wait until the storm passed. It seemed foolish to continue riding into what appeared to be worsening conditions. As I was turning, the motorcycle was nearly blown off the road by a severe blast of wind. The increasing size of the hailstones was evident from the sound of them bouncing off my helmet. I could feel the pellets through the thick, protective skin of the Aerostich. Lightning struck very close by and visibility dropped to less than a hundred feet. Now the hailstones were larger, approaching the size of golf balls. Thinking again about the danger of a tornado, I wanted to be off the motorcycle and in as safe a position as I could find.

I saw an opportunity to move the bike off the highway to an area used to stockpile gravel, apparently for use by the highway department to spread on icy highways in the winter. Any alternative seemed better than continuing to be on the road on the motorcycle. I parked the bike heading north so that it leaned into the wind on its sidestand.

There was a shallow trench running parallel to each side of the highway. Recalling that it's safer to be in a depression in the event of a tornado, I headed for the trench. The wind at my back, I fought against it to resist being blown into the trench.

The storm raged as I sat in the gully in full riding gear. I got down as low as I could without entering the rising water. At least I knew I would be able to survive anything short of a tornado. I jumped, startled once again at the sound of a close thunderclap and brightness all around. I could smell ozone in the air. A shudder of fear enveloped my body, from head to toe.

"What is there to be afraid of?" I thought. "The chances of being struck by lightning are probably infinitesimal now that I'm safely away from the motorcycle. And I'm not going to get any wetter by sitting here."

I tried to find humor in the situation. Sometimes I amaze myself when forced to acknowledge that in some bizarre way, I enjoy circumstances such as this. I enjoy every phenomenon nature proffers, including the fury and severity of her storms. They're an important part of a totality that I don't like to avoid. I'd have missed something important if I'd remained in Augusta while the storm passed. I'd have missed the excitement. I'd have missed the purity and genuineness of this magnificent event.

I've often tried to describe the difference between driving a car and riding a motorcycle. I've compared driving to looking at scenery go by, while riding allows you to be part of the picture. Senses are aroused by the wind, the smells of the forests and the fields, and the sound of the vehicle moving against the road.

I've always wanted to experience a long voyage, perhaps around the world, in a small boat. I've been told that being in a severe storm at sea is a fearsome thing, and I'm sure it is. I'm sure it's much more fearsome than sitting in a ditch beside a rural Montana highway during a summer thunderstorm. But this does nicely for now.

Just as I turned to see if the motorcycle was still upright, a car approached slowly from the south, passed the motorcycle, and stopped in the highway. The car sat there for a minute or two, the driver apparently wondering about the abandoned motorcycle. Finally the backup lights were illuminated as the driver shifted into reverse and backed slowly into the parking area near the motorcycle. I heard a few short blasts of the car's horn.

I rose from my position in the ditch and walked toward the parked car. The wind was so strong that I had to make a concerted effort to lean into it to cover the short distance to the car. I was forced back a step, braced myself, and proceeded again toward the passenger side of the car.

The side windows of the car were clouded, preventing me from seeing inside. I didn't know if I could be seen. I tapped on the windshield and waited a few moments, then opened the door and saw a young woman, probably no older than 25, motioning for me to get into the car with her.

"Get in here! Get out of this storm!" the woman pleaded.

I opened my face shield all the way so she could see my face.

"Thanks a million for stopping, but I'm really all right," I replied. "I'm dry and safe with this gear on. If I join you, I'll just get your car wet and muddy."

"Don't worry about it," she insisted. "Just get in!"

I thanked her again, emphasizing once again how generous it was of her to stop, and assuring her that I would be fine.

"Are you *sure?*" she insisted, before driving off.

"Yes, I'm sure. Please don't worry about me. And thanks again."

As she pulled onto the highway and proceeded toward Augusta, I returned to the gully and resumed my previous position. I thought about how unusual it would seem to people in populated areas of the country for a young woman to stop in such a desolate area to render assistance to an unknown motorcyclist.

A few minutes later, another passing car slowed as it approached the motorcycle, stopped on the highway, and turned into the parking area. This time I walked to the car without hesitation. As I approached, a woman in her mid-thirties reached across the seat and pushed the passenger door open.

"Are you alright? Can I help you?" she asked.

"Thank you for stopping," I shouted over the sound of the wind and the rain. It was no longer hailing, but the heavy wind and rain persisted.

"You folks out here are *incredible.*" I continued. "Aren't you concerned about stopping for a stranger in a place like this?"

She appeared surprised that I would ask such a question while the storm raged around us.

"Forget about *that,*" she insisted. "Are you sure I can't help you? Would you like to sit in the car while this thing blows over?"

"Thanks, but the hail has stopped and these furious storms don't generally last long. I think it's about done with, and I'm fine in this outfit," I replied as I pointed to my suit.

"OK, but be real careful out here," she implored, as she pulled away.

"This must be evidence of some sort of code of conduct that people who live in remote, sparsely-populated areas observe," I thought, as she pulled away.

The wind seemed to decrease and the rain lessened a bit. As I walked toward the motorcycle, I could hear the approach of yet another vehicle as it crunched the gravel of the parking lot. I turned as a large van approached.

"I can't believe this," I thought. "Now a van. And I suppose this time I'm going to meet a den of Girl Scouts."

The door of the van slid open. Now the wind and rain had almost stopped. An elderly woman was operating the sliding door, apparently accompanied in the rear seat by her husband. A younger man was behind the steering wheel and a woman about his age was in the front passenger seat.

"My God, wasn't that storm just *awful!*" the elderly woman exclaimed. "Was it bad here too? Are you OK?"

"Bad here too?" I asked. "Yes, it was a real humdinger," I laughed. "I thought the wind was going to blow my motorcycle over. And the hail was pretty large there for a while."

"It's a good thing you weren't back down the road a piece," she continued, pointing back over her shoulder with her thumb. "That hail was so heavy the road was white with it. We thought we had been in a snowstorm, the ground was so white."

"Sounds like I did the right thing to stop here then. I was heading south and turned around to see if I could make it back to Augusta. Guess I'll continue on my way, now that it's blown over."

My leather gloves were drenched. I considered replacing them with a dry pair, then decided to continue with the wet ones. I didn't see the point in changing them until it stopped raining.

I hit the switch to insure that my heated handgrips were turned to the highest setting, then plugged in my electric vest. I turned the bike around and continued south. I've learned that electric heat can stave off discomfort when you're wet, provided you get settled into a position and don't shift around. You're still wet, but at least you're being warmed by moisture that's been heated by the electrics. But if you shift your body around at all and disturb the "cling" that's sticking your wet clothes to your body, you'll suffer an immediate chill until you've settled down again.

The same goes for gloves. As long as you maintain a constant pressure and position on the handlebars, the heated grips will keep your hands warm and comfortable, even when you're wet. But remove your hands from the grips to adjust something, and they'll be chilled for a while.

After a few miles, the shoulder of the road turned white, where the hail hadn't yet melted. A little further, the road, too, turned white and I concentrated on keeping my tires in the black section of the road where the tires of other vehicles had cleared the ice. I had never before seen such vivid evidence of a hailstorm. I was fortunate to have stopped when I did, rather than to have continued into what apparently was much more severe weather than I had experienced.

As I cautiously negotiated my way through the slick, hail-strewn highway, I thought about the incredible good fortune I've enjoyed in my ten-year riding career. I wondered if God doesn't have a soft spot in his heart for motorcyclists.

Before the start of several endurance rallies in which I've participated, a member of a Christian motorcycle organization will deliver a benediction. During one such benediction, the evangelist assured us that God does indeed love motorcyclists. He prayed that an angel would be assigned to sit with each rider throughout the rally to protect him from harm. Although it's been years since I've attended church, I've often felt that I must have a guardian angel looking after me.

I was reminded of an experience that Jan Cutler had during a ride from Flagstaff, Arizona, to the Oregon coast. I was so impressed by Jan's story that I asked him to document his recollection of it for me.

The ride to the Oregon coast was time-constrained. Owing to schedules and duties, I had only four days to ride from Flagstaff to the Oregon coast and return.

As the miles passed, I remember only that there was heightened perception of smells, colors, sound—the barriers of self were coming down and exposing me to the world around. Thirty-eight hours without sleep, yet, I was not fatigued—the discovery of the ride was energizing. There would be time for sleeping later.

Entering a small valley west of Hwy 97, I recall that the midday sun had changed the shadows of the trees lining the road. A few minutes later I would be cresting the hill ahead. I recall, too, there was a slight color shift as if someone turned the intensity knob on the surrounding scenery. Then it happened, an experience that would alter forever my perception of the symbiosis of man, machine, and life in general.

As if in a dream, I hovered briefly high above the Beemer looking directly down on the rider—me! There was no feeling of fear or disorientation, in fact, the unusual part of the episode was that it felt calming and natural. Ahead, over the rise, I could see from my vantage point above the bike that a logging truck had overturned, scattering its load along the road. It hadn't come to a rest yet; the truck was on its right side, sliding, while disgorging logs in all directions. Then I was back on the bike, ascending the grade and approaching the crest.

Immediately, I slowed and shifted down to 4th, 3rd, 2nd in rapid succession. I crested the hill and still had to brake to avoid a log that was crosswise in the middle of my lane. There was no path around the obstacles, the shoulder was blocked, and both lanes were impassable.

The driver of the truck was pulling himself out of the cab—the accident had happened a moment before I arrived. The driver had minor injuries and was concerned about getting flares out to warn approaching drivers, which we did immediately. He marveled that I avoided hitting the logs. I was still sorting it out.

To the few with whom I have shared this story, all manner of conjecture and explanations have been offered. ESP, clairvoyance, good vibrations, a figment of a fatigued mind—I reject none of these out of hand, they may all be part of it. I only know what occurred and I can add that similar things have happened since, although not as dramatic. And, they have occurred under similar circumstances.

The motorcycle is probably just another door amongst countless that we can pass through and see or experience the other side. Yet in this scenario it was me, a beloved machine, and a blissful ride that opened my perception to wider possibilities and lead me to write these lines:

Questions, so many questions
And in their answering
The awesome suggestions
Of more and better questions

As I reflected on such thoughts on this lonely road in Montana, the rain resumed. Long branches of lightning arched across the distant sky to the south. The streaks of lightning looked like fingers, reaching blindly for something to grasp.

To my right, a herd of cattle, perhaps fifty head, were standing single file along the fence, as if pushed there by the westerly wind. Five minutes later, another herd was huddled together on the western side of a small hill running parallel to the highway, as if seeking shelter from the wind.

Several miles further, I entered I-15 and exited at Wolf Creek, only two miles from where I got on. By now my riding suit had leaked sufficiently that I wanted to change into dry clothes. I stopped at a small filling station and general store.

After refueling, I pushed the motorcycle away from the station's only set of gasoline pumps and took some dry clothing from the saddlebag and a small notepad and pen from my tank bag.

"Might as well use this opportunity to hang around a bit and catch up on some note-taking," I thought. I welcomed the idea of being warm for a while, of having something to eat, and of being able to capture the events of the trip from Edmonton.

I walked into the small store carrying my helmet, gloves, dry clothing, and notebook.

"Which direction are you coming from?" the clerk asked as I offered the charge card.

"South on 287," I answered. "I came through Choteau and Augusta."

"Do you know if they had power when you came through? I heard power was out up there because of one hellish storm."

"I can attest to the storm. It hit the towns after I passed through. I'm not surprised about the power loss. I thought I was in a typhoon. I had to park the bike and sit it out to keep from being blown off the road."

"Well, you're welcome to stay in here and warm up. You stay as long as you like."

As the clerk was completing our transaction, a customer entered the store. He studied me briefly, then chuckled.

"Hey, where's your spaceship? You look like Buzz Aldridge or somebody," he smiled. "Does that outfit keep you dry in a squall like this?" he asked, motioning to my Aerostich suit.

"Yes, it does," I lied. My response was defensive and automatic. "I must look like an idiot," I thought, standing here with an armful of dry clothing as I prepared to use the bathroom to change. I realized that I was acting like so many riders who, after shelling out more than 700 bucks for one of these suits, then feel obligated to defend it in spite of an obvious shortcoming. I decided to try to recover, to disguise a dishonest answer and hope that it would be interpreted as sarcasm.

"Of course, that's why I'm standing here about to use the restroom to change into dry clothes." I extended the hand that was carrying the dry clothes slightly. "We call these things Aeroleaks," I laughed, nodding my head downward toward my riding outfit. Then I realized that a non-rider wouldn't understand this remark. It was just as well, since I don't enjoy disparaging the Aerostich. It's too good a product, save its one shortcoming, to deserve derision.

The man acknowledged my response with laughter, shook his head, and walked to the coffee machine.

I changed into dry clothes and examined the shelves for something to eat. I was still trying to observe the improved eating habits I had adopted in preparation for the 7/49, so I passed on the hotdogs that were revolving on the rotisserie at the end of the counter. I selected two packages of strawberry-flavored, no-fat Fig Newtons and removed a cold bottle of spring water from the cooler. The clerk was seated at a small table with the man who had asked about my "astronaut gear," along with a second clerk. She interrupted their conversation to let me pay for my purchase, then returned to her seat at the table to continue their conversation. I walked to a counter on the opposite side of the room, opened my notebook, and started to scribble notes about the day's journey.

After about a half-hour the rain stopped. I called Barbara to report that the delay caused by the weather would prevent me from arriving in Colorado in time for my meeting with Randell. He and I had agreed to communicate any changes in our plans through her. I thanked the clerks for their hospitality and returned to the motorcycle. I retrieved my last pair of dry gloves and wedged the wet ones beneath the bungee cords securing a duffel bag to one of the saddlebags.

I continued south on I-15 to Helena, then took 287 again and headed for the Idaho border. If I was going to meet Randell in Buena Vista by tomorrow morning, I would have to ride through the night, perhaps grabbing a two-hour nap at a rest area along the way.

My route into Idaho and then east into Wyoming had been planned to avoid holiday traffic at Yellowstone National Park and the most heavily-visited areas of the Tetons. I followed Route 20 to Ashton, Idaho, and Route 33 to Victor, then continued east to Jackson, Wyoming, via the Teton Pass. I avoided most vacation travelers by crossing the Tetons from the west, rather than taking the more heavily traveled John D. Rockefeller Jr. Memorial Highway that extends southward from Yellowstone.

The Grand Tetons

The Grand Tetons dominate the landscape at Jackson, Wyoming. I had been to Jackson many times, but had never ridden through the Grand Tetons. I had been looking forward to the opportunity to cross this imposing range ever since I'd begun planning my return trip to Texas.

As I crossed the border, entered Wyoming, and began my climb toward Teton Pass, I was overcome with an extraordinary sense of happiness and serenity. I welcomed the chilly mountain air and the solitude the ride provided. I celebrated each twist and turn in the highway as I shifted my weight and altered pressure on the handlebars. It was just after midnight and the PIAA driving lights had been blazing brightly for a half-hour, illuminating the mountain road and mitigating the dangers of riding such a road at high speed at night. I increased my speed and leaned into the sharp curves, riding more aggressively than at any time since approaching Alaska three weeks earlier.

As my speed and altitude rose, so too, did my spirits. I opened the throttle even more, clearly challenged now by the twists and turns as I was propelled toward the top of the mountain. I wanted to race to the summit as quickly as I could, then stop to smell the roses. I had been rushing since leaving Edmonton. I wanted to indulge in private, quiet thoughts, totally undisturbed high in these majestic mountains. I wanted to reflect on how my abundant treasure of experiences had been multiplied by the events of the last several weeks.

As the motorcycle catapulted me toward the peak, there were signs warning that stopping is forbidden. At the summit, there's an area for trucks to stop to test their brakes before descending the steep downgrade ahead. I glanced up and was astounded at the brightness and clarity of the stars. I pulled to the side of the road, into the brake test area. I didn't want to miss this opportunity to look at the stars right then and there.

I removed my gloves and helmet and looked at the heavens. The sky never looked brighter or more beautiful. The magnificent, motionless Milky Way flowed silently toward the southern sky like a pearly, opalescent river. Scorpio was in full view, with Antares, the "Fourth of July Star," twinkling red at the heart of the constellation, the most prominent star in the southern sky.

"How fortunate," I thought. "How fortunate to have the opportunity to view the star tonight, only minutes into the Fourth of July—the day of the year when Antares is at its brightest.

To the north I saw the Big Dipper, and directly overhead, blue Vega, the fourth brightest star, anchoring one corner of the Great Triangle used by ancient mariners for navigation.

I always think about how much nicer it would be for Barbara to be with me to share moments like this. She often rides with me, although she never rides on endurance events.

I thought back to the 1995 dinner for Iron Butt Rally contestants in Salt Lake City.

"The Iron Butt Rally will change your lives," rallymaster Steve Chalmers told the group.

At the time I thought the statement was melodramatic. Now, I believe it was prophetic. Endurance riding has had a more dramatic impact on my life than motorcycling by itself ever could. I've developed friendships with members of the endurance riding community that are deeper and more genuine than any that I've experienced over the years.

I've had a lifetime of experiences crammed into the three years since my first Iron Butt Rally in 1995. I've lived a life rich

Steve
Chalmers and
Ron Major
discuss the
possibilities in
the 1995 Iron
Butt (photo by
Suzy Johnson).

in the kind of experiences that most people can find only by reading novels or watching movies. The 7/49 in particular was a "once-in-a-lifetime" experience that I'll never forget. I reflected back on a message that I received from Jack Tollett shortly after my 7/49 ride was over:

Ron,

During our lives we all dream of doing something truly outstanding. For some it may be to climb Mt. Everest, others might dream of sailing around the world alone, while others fantasize about winning the Indy 500. Few of us get a chance to live out those dreams. You are indeed a fortunate man to have been able to fulfill one of yours. For that alone you deserve our congratulations and respect, but for allowing us to "travel" along with you and to be part of your dream, you deserve our heartfelt thanks.

Thank you, Ron.

Jack Tollett

Colorado

When I arrived at the designated meeting spot at a motel in Buena Vista, I called Barbara and learned that Randell had given up on me. Because of my delay and the continuing bad weather, he had headed for home.

I was exhausted from the long ride and asked about a room at the motel. Because of the holiday weekend, all rooms in the area were taken.

I decided to continue homeward myself and stop at the first motel displaying a vacancy sign. My opportunity came in Poncha Springs, as I secured the last available room at a small, independently-operated motel. The clerk, a middle-aged man who I surmised was the owner of the motel, was prepared for guests on motorcycles.

"Let me follow you to your cabin," he offered. "I'd like to provide a block of wood for your sidestand. The asphalt here is soft and sometimes motorcycles sink into it. I'll bring you a bucket with some rags in case you want to clean your bike." This was a polite way of suggesting I not use the motel towels and linen for that purpose.

In the interest of protecting the image of motorcyclists, I don't use motel towels to check my oil or clean grease from the bike. I appreciate it when motels volunteer the use of rags.

I was asleep by 2:00 p.m., but woke five hours later and decided to make a non-stop run for home. "This motel operator will be thrilled," I thought. "He'll have no trouble renting the room again, considering how booked everything is."

I walked to the office to check out.

"If you can get the room serviced, you can get it rented again this evening," I said, as I handed him the key to the room.

"Sure, I'll get it fixed up myself. When you checked in, didn't you tell me you rode all the way from Canada?"

"Yes, that's right. And before that, I visited all 48 contiguous states and Alaska," I replied.

"*Really!* Wow. That must have taken some time."

"It took more than a week," I replied.

"Yeah. I guess so," the clerk chuckled.

13

Epilogue

After a thorough validation by the Iron Butt Association, my ride was certified as taking six days, thirty-one minutes for the 48 states, and seven days, twenty minutes for 49 states. The nineteen-minute discrepancy between these official times and my assumptions after the ride is attributed to my misunderstanding how the starting time was to be calculated. I had assumed that the clock would start in Maine when I purchased gasoline, rather than when the witnesses signed the forms. I obviously should have purchased the gasoline before obtaining the witness signatures.

I'd promised the official witnesses a special memento to commemorate the event. I commissioned a pin with a reproduction of the North American continent, with my route identified. I've provided one to each of the supporters who turned out to meet me, in addition to the official witnesses.

Others Accomplishments
One of the most rewarding aspects of my adventure was totally unexpected when the trip was planned. I didn't anticipate how the event would become such a personal experience to those who helped me and to those who followed the progress of the ride on the Internet. Just as the sport has changed my life, it seems that many other lives have been influenced in some small way by my ride.

In December, I received a note from Norm Babcock after he learned that he and Linda had won the BMW Motorcycle Owners Association high-mileage contest for the preceding six-month period. Linda had won the ladies category with almost 40,000 miles, and Norm won the men's category with nearly 50,000. This was the first time a husband and wife team had captured the awards. The 7/49 was a small part of their mileage achievement.

Shane Smith, a top finisher in the 1997 Iron Butt Rally, and his wife Karen, were our houseguests a few months after my ride. Shane related the story of how he and Fran Crane rode to Hyder together shortly after I completed my ride.

Shane was at Laguna Seca on his new motorcycle to attend the World Super Bike Race. As Alaska was the only state he had not visited on his previous motorcycle, he decided a trip to Hyder would be a fitting way to break in the new bike. He admitted that the idea was inspired, at least in part, by my recent ride. Fran had never been to Alaska and offered to accompany him.

"When we arrived in Hyder, several people asked if I had heard about the guy who was here a few weeks ago after setting a new record for visiting 49 of the states," Shane reported.

"I certainly *have* heard of him," Shane replied. "He's a good friend of mine and I'll be staying at his house and eating a lot of barbecue with him in a few weeks."

"Ron, the people of Hyder asked me to be sure to tell you that you're well-known and fondly remembered in Hyder," Shane added.

Shane and Fran's last-minute decision to make the ride demonstrates the spontaneity that characterizes the behavior of so many riders in the group.

"I remember Fran talking at breakfast about how most people would have planned for months to ride to Hyder," Shane related. "We just decided over a phone call and it was a done deal. No big plans, just go ride to Hyder. We had a great time."

Jerry Harris, who rode with me from Santa Fe to Albuquerque, became so excited about the idea of riding greater distances than he had ridden before that he started his first 1,000-

mile day before I even finished the 48-state portion of my ride. After completing the SaddleSore, Jerry decided that neither the Harley nor his BMW R1100RSL was what he wanted for serious long-distance riding, so he began searching for a new K1100LT. He found one in California, which provided him an excuse to perform another SaddleSore 1000.

Jerry wrote:

The info from you and the other LD riders was invaluable in allowing me to get started. Diet, hydration, timing, or pacing the ride. Even the roadside "Iron Butt Motel." What have I learned? I have mastered the 1-hour sleep on a picnic table. I wake after 1 hour without a Screaming Meanie. I can sleep sitting on the bike leaning over the tank (if the local Sheriffs would just stop waking me up to see if I'm OK). I've learned to avoid sleeping alongside my bike at the boat ramp parking lot on highway 50 east of Fallon, NV, at 1:00 a.m. due to massive mosquito bites on my face and hands after an hour. The swelling and itching kept me awake for the next week and was miserable under leather gloves going to Montana. I learned that rest areas have sprinklers that go on in the middle of the night, so catching an hour of sleep should take that into account, or wet clothes are miserable to ride in. I can do 5-minute gas stops. I can live on bananas and granola bars with a few hard candies and enough water. Power bars are almost impossible to swallow. First Gear suits cover a wide temperature range, but melt on the exhaust like anything else.

I learned that I am old enough and gray enough to avoid speeding tickets by stopping the bike, stepping off, taking off my helmet, and starting a conversation with the LEO (3 escapes in the last few months). I think the technique worked for you a time or two on the 7/49.

After my ride, Bryce Ulrich did his own 49-state ride, although he took eight months to do it. His ultimate goal was to visit all 50 states, however. In November, I had dinner with Bryce, Marie, Joe Zulaski, and Ron Smith. Bryce and Marie had recently returned from Hawaii, where they rented a motorcycle to complete the 50-state objective. Dr. Marie Grohman is now a certified motorcycle junkie, having received her license in October, 1998.

At the end of the summer, Michigan witness Glenn Pancoast completed his own 48-state ride in "eight days and a whole bunch of hours."

One month after the completion of my ride, Bill Koehler wrote me about his first IBA qualifying ride.

Ron,

Thanks for the 7/49 witness pin. It looks great next to the Iron Butt pin on the stich.

Being part of your 7/49 event made a real change in my riding habits. Prior to meeting you, I typically rode 3–4k per year. Since I have found the Iron Butt and witnessed for you, it has completely changed my riding habits.

This year I have logged 22k miles!! Also, prior to your 7/49, I thought about doing a SaddleSore 1000 many times but convinced myself it was too hard. Then, the day I rode out to meet you, I took the longgggg way home and logged about 800 miles. I didn't plan this, but it hit me: if Ron can do all 49 states in seven days, I surely can do 1,000 miles. Soon after that I did my first official SaddleSore 1000. Without a doubt, it was one of the best days of my life. Since then I have done many unofficial 1,000-mile days and am loving it.

It doesn't stop there. When I show up to work at 10:00 a.m., they know what I have been up to and everyone wants to know what states I have been in since I left my house. Often I have ridden 250 miles to get to work, which normally should be 50 miles.

All my friends and family think I am crazy when, say, I go to Ohio and back just for the hell of it.

So, thanks Ron, for the inspiration and the pin to show off.

Jack Baird, owner of Crocodile Motor Sports in Kennewick, Washington, wrote:

Ron,

Congratulations on the ride!!! It's because of Warchild, and people like you that have just inspired me to join the Iron Butt Association. With the help of Dale, I just completed the SaddleSore 1000. It was a great privilege to have you in my dealership in Washington on your way to setting the record. I wish I could have asked you some questions, but in light of it all, I managed to restrain myself. Anyway, I plan to compete in the 2001 Iron Butt. Your book inspired that. I just got it in the mail, and already I have read it cover to cover.

The letter you wrote is proudly displayed in a frame at this dealership. I can't thank you enough.

Ride on. Soon they will have verified all of the info I have sent them on my SaddleSore 1000, an IBA member. I hope to see you at some of the events I will be attending in the future.

And Gary Dehner sent the following message:

Maybe I'm just too old or wise to start into racing as I once did with MGs and Porsches but I seem to have caught the "let's go for a ride" and they turn into a 350-mile jaunt or recently a 1,600-mile weekend, etc. Maybe it was Christian's involvement in your 7/49 success or ?? Anyway I'm signed up to do the Tarbutt and will do a SaddleSore before. Then off to the Feast in the East . . .

All of this without a clue (except from your book and the Iron Butt web site) and on a 92 Virago 750. It does have a Mustang seat, driving lights, a throttle lock, and some odds and ends. It's what I've got . . . for the time being.

Any suggestions?

Mark Gawecki, a witness in Michigan, sent the following message:

Dear Ron,

. . . Your recent 7/48/49 has been inspirational to us. During the 4th of July weekend we did a SaddleSore 1000, circumnavigating Lake Michigan. Tomorrow we

*leave for a trip to Yellowstone to try to capture nine
states in the National Park 50 / 25 / 12 Rally.*

*Perhaps by next year we'll have more in common to
talk about.*

Hope it cools down for your BBQ.

Jeff Gordy, who accompanied me from Hattiesburg, Mississippi, to the Louisiana State line, wrote:

*I am sure you have heard this plenty of times by now,
but congratulations!!!!!!!*

*Sorry I was your only fan in Mississippi to show for
the ride. I feel honored to have been a small part in
your ride of a lifetime. You have inspired me, and
many more, to set a higher goal with this madness we
all cannot get enough of. From the time I met you and
other long-distance riders at Shane Smith's this spring
I have pushed my distance a bit further on every ride. I
only hope to follow in the same path that you have
laid . . .*

Bryan Moody, one of several volunteers who I stood up in
North Carolina during the first day of the ride, wrote:

Ron,

*Congratulations on your 7 / 49. It has really inspired
me to further my riding experiences. As a matter of
fact, I did a BBG on Saturday just to get in the spirit
of things. Sorry that Jerry Clemmons, Hank Rowland,
LD Holland, and I missed you in NC but I will see you
at the Feast in the East in October.*

Way to go!

Fellow Texan Norm Grills wrote:

*OK, I got the SaddleSore 1,000-mile ride under my
belt and I'm hooked! So much so that I got the ol' Map
n Go out and laid out a 1,500- and a 2,000-mile ride.
Figure I'll go for the Bun Burner Gold in October when
it cools down and save the 2,000 for later.*

*I'm also seriously considering the Butt Lite 5K. So
much so that I went out today and committed to a '94*

*K1100 LT with 18k miles on it. My '85 K/RT with 78k
miles (the miles didn't worry me) was only getting 35
mpg and that was creating a lot of fuel stops. Also, the
'85 is not as ergonomically suitable as the '94 . . .*

*Darn you, Ron Ayres. Look what you have gone and
done! (Just kidding!!!!!).*

*I was looking for a new twist to motorcycling. I had
been considering doing some GS riding until I heard
Ron talk at one of our club socials and then followed
his progress on the historic 7/49. Then I realized what
I was supposed to do, ride long distances—not that I
am in the same league with Ron, mind you . . .*

On June 23, I received a message from Joe Zulaski, informing me of his plans to do some endurance riding. Joe closed his
letter with a suggested title for this book:

*One question before I go. Are you going to write a book
about your 7/49 adventure? If so, put me down for a
copy when they come out. Curious what you'll call it.
"Against the Clock?"*

Neither Joe nor I knew it at the time, but Dan Kennedy and
his staff at Whitehorse Press had a brainstorming session and
came up with the same name.

Jackie Mosmiller, one of my Maryland witnesses wrote:

*It was a thrill meeting you and being able to follow
you on the 'net. I would race to work and check in and
then check again before I went home. I'd call John and
read the messages and then print everything out for
him to read later and for us to keep. My printer died
on the last two legs, so I called my accountant and had
him print it for me. I've tried to get everyone involved.*

*My daughter thought I was nuts. Customers would
come in and want to know how that guy was doing on
his bike. I think the absolute worst was not actually
riding with you on a motorcycle. John came up with
the idea of a sidecar so we could try it non-stop. I'm
not so sure he could sleep with my driving. Well, it
sure has been fun for us. Your son seems to be as nice
as you. The one thing that came out of everything I
read was what a nice person you are no matter the*

*weather, the problems, or whatever. Thank you for
letting us be a part of your dream . . .*

Ed Lutz, a friend who I had met at an endurance rally in
Nevada wrote:

*It was incredible being able to follow you around the
country. It gave my wife a better understanding of just
what this endurance thing is all about. She still thinks
I'm nuts, but she's got a better understanding of what
happens. "What do you mean he's in Alaska! He just
left Needles!!!"*

Eight months after my ride, I was at a conference in Florida
with one of my Texas witnesses, Dan Vanlandingham. While we
were having dinner, Dan had me in stitches as he related his
story of acquiring the large blister on his butt after riding to
Texarkana from Houston. When I finally stopped laughing, I
told Dan about how I met Oly in North Dakota and how he decided to skip work in order to ride with me through North Dakota, Montana, South Dakota, Wyoming, and Nebraska.

"Ron, that event provided a whole lot of people, including
me, with a reason to get out and have a great time," Dan as-
serted. "I hadn't had such a great time in ages. I really enjoyed
meeting the guys at the Texarkana checkpoint. How else could I
have ever met such a cast of characters?

"And look at your own experience," Dan continued. "Running into Oly like that had to have been a great unexpected bonus."

It was indeed, but not all endings are perfect.

On a Sadder Note

Gary Olson, who spontaneously joined me for a thousand miles
of my ride, lost his job as a pipe-fitter apprentice. "Oly" wrote to
tell me that his supervisor didn't appreciate his last-minute decision to pass up work for the opportunity to ride with me
through North Dakota, Montana, South Dakota, Wyoming, and
Nebraska. I expressed my sympathy to Oly, but he insists he
would do the same thing if he had to do it over again. A kindred
spirit, indeed. As soon as I returned home, I sent him a signed
copy of *Against the Wind.*

Jack Baird and Dale Wilson were on their way to a rally in Gerlach, Nevada, when Jack lost control of his motorcycle and ran off the road. He was hospitalized. Shortly before Christmas, I wrote and asked Jack how he was doing. He replied:

Hi Ron,

I am progressing along just fine. I am looking forward to the time when my Doctor says, "It's time to start physical therapy, Jack." I'm hoping that will be on New Years Eve when I go back for re-evaluation. Until then, I just tool around in this wheelchair. It would appear that I have some neurological damage as well. That will keep me out of the driver's seat of a car, and off the seat of a bike for about a year. Drat the luck!!!

The good news is that I will still be able to be useful in the '99 Butt. I am the northwest checkpoint. It's not all bad. I will be in great shape for the 2001 Butt! I'm looking forward to that.

Ron, from me and my family to you and yours . . . Merry Christmas and a Happy New Year.

Thanks for your concern.

See you again one day, my friend.

Jack Baird

Shortly after my ride, I received a message from Jan Cutler, informing me that he would be closing Reno BMW. A few weeks later I received a package from him—a new set of deer whistles.

Off to Africa

In February, 1999, I relocated to Johannesburg to accept the position of Chief Executive Officer, EDS Africa. Barbara was under contract with a college in Dallas until May and plans to join me in Johannesburg after she fulfils her teaching commitment. Although I had to cancel many endurance riding activities that I had planned for 1999, I promised not to let my new assignment interfere with the 1999 Iron Butt Rally. As this book goes to press, I'm planning to be there.

I'll miss my active participation with the endurance riding community for the next few years, but I'm looking forward to being introduced to a new, different dimension. Initial indications are that there is some great riding available in Africa.

One Year Later

Barbara and I enjoyed Hyder so much that we announced plans to return for a celebration one year later. Linda Babcock suggested we name the event "Hyder Seek." Although Linda, her husband Norm, and six other riders attended the event, my South African assignment prevented Barbara and me from being there.

Since we couldn't be in Hyder, we did the next best thing. As the Hyder group was having dinner at the Sealaska Inn, we called from South Africa to participate vicariously. As the phone passed among the attendees, I learned that the group was celebrating both my ride and Vince Kretzul's "Moose Encounter."

"Being in Hyder, eating steak, drinking beer with friends, and talking to a friend from the other side of the planet," Vince commented, "it just doesn't get any better than this. Wish you were here."

With any luck, Barbara and I will make "Hyder Seek 2000."

14
Afterword

One of the questions I'm frequently asked by riders who would like to participate in long-distance riding is how I handle the concerns my wife has about my participation in it. I'm very fortunate for Barbara's attitude. I've asked her to summarize it.

I would be devastated if anything ever happened to Ron, but this doesn't preclude me from respecting his right to decide for himself what kind of risks he wants to take, or what level of adventure he wants in his life. If it would make me happier if he gave up riding, but would diminish his happiness, on what basis could I decide that my happiness is more important than his?

Also, I want him to be the person he is. My favorite quote sums this up: "Never destroy any aspect of personality, for what you think is the wild branch may be the heart of the tree."

I worry a lot and I pray a lot when Ron is on a long ride, but I also believe in fate. As human beings, we give ourselves too much credit for being able to control things. Ron acknowledges that being on a motorcycle is more dangerous than being at home in an easy chair, but if something bad is going to happen, it can happen even if you are doing something completely routine and safe. What is meant to be, will be.

On the positive side, I've been a beneficiary of Ron's sport. I've met some of the most interesting, original, and colorful characters of my life. Ron has made some very good friends who have demonstrated they would do anything for him. I wouldn't trade this for anything.

Appendix A
7/49 Witnesses

Because of difficulties during the first day, I canceled my planned Tennessee, North Carolina, and South Carolina checkpoints. I want to offer special thanks to my friends at those checkpoints for being there for most of the night and early morning, even though I didn't make it.

Checkpoint	Witness	Home Town
Tennessee	Kelly Council	Newbern, TN
	Jim Culp	Johnson City, TN
	Geoffrey Greene	Knoxville, TN
	Donald Warren	Cleveland, TN
North Carolina	Jerry Clemmons	Gastonia, NC
	Gregg Garner	Charlotte, NC
	LD Holland	Denver, NC
	Bryan Moody	Greensboro, NC
	Hank Rowland	Morganton, NC
South Carolina	Wally Jordan	Prescott, AZ
	Joel Langlois	Hendersonville, NC

CHECKPOINT VOLUNTEERS

Date, Time, Checkpoint	Witness	Home Town
Sunday June 7, 6:07 p.m., Kittery, Maine	Howard Chain	Nashua, NH
	John McKay	Canterbury, NH
	Jeff Watts	Westbrook, ME
Sunday, June 7, 6:30 p.m., Portsmouth, New Hampshire	Todd Crowley	Windham, NH
	Ed Farrell	Augusta, ME
	Jeff Small	Manchester, ME
Sunday, June 7, 7:45 p.m., Marlborough, Massachusetts	Jeffrey Luke	Bondsville, MA
	Jamison Luke	North Attleboro, MA
	Camela Pryor	North Attleboro, MA
Sunday, June 7, 8:20 p.m., Woonsocket, Rhode Island	Tom Maloney	Wakefield, RI
	Brian Roth	Middletown, RI
	Michael Thrasher	Nashua, NH
Sunday, June 7, 11:00 p.m., Brattleboro, Vermont	Kathleen Boyer	Montague, MA
	Tom Mangieri	Antrim, NH
	Harry Pendexter	Center Conway, NH
Monday, June 8, 1:30 a.m., Stamford, Connecticut	Maurice Donini	Milford, CT
	Bill Kramer	Drums, PA
	Berti Levy	Ft. Lee, NJ
	Joe Xiques	Bogota, NJ
Monday, June 8, 2:15 a.m., Bronx, New York	Jeffrey Hicken	New York, NY
	Gary Johnson	Bronx, NY
	Keith Sproul	North Brunswick, NJ
	Mark Sproul	North Brunswick, NJ
Monday, June 8, 4:05 a.m., Runnemede, New Jersey	Walter Barlow	Spotswood, NJ
	Al Spilotras	Highland Lakes, NJ
Monday, June 8, 5:08 a.m., Newark, Delaware	Chris BeHanna	Kintnersville, PA
	Tom Coradeschi	Hackettstown, NJ
	Harold Gantz	Mt. Laurel, NJ
Monday, June 8, 6:33 a.m., Mt. Airy, Maryland	Louis Caplan	Alexandria, VA
	Diane Donaldson	Adelphi, MD
	John Mosmiller	Abington, MD
	Jackie Mosmiller	Abington, MD
Monday, June 8, 7:25 a.m., Marlowe, West Virginia	Leon Begeman	Dale City, VA
	Gary Castleman	Martinsburg, WV
	John Laurenson	St. Augustine, FL
	Leonard Roy	Upper Marlboro, MD

Date, Time, Checkpoint	Witness	Home Town
Monday, June 8, 8:46 a.m., Bedford, Pennsylvania	Michael Galloway	Altoona, PA
	Fred Johns	Youngstown, OH
	Bill Koehler	Saylorsburg, PA
Monday, June 8, 2:27 p.m., Elyria, Ohio	Bill Carson	Canton, OH
	Michael Cox	University Heights, OH
	Jerry Flynn	Lebanon, OH
	Brian Mehosky	Walton Hills, OH
Monday, June 8, 4:14 p.m., Ottawa Lake, Michigan	Art Holland	Westland, MI
	Jim Kraus	DeWitt, MI
	Glenn Pancoast	Lansing, MI
	Bobb Todd	Owen Sound, Ontario
Monday, June 8, 8:03 p.m., Lawrenceburg, Indiana	Mitch Comstock	Cincinnati, OH
	Robert Evans	Hammond, IN
	George Herren	Cincinnati, OH
	Mary Sue Johnson	Griffith, IN
	Michael Murphy	Belleville, IL
	James Warren	Plainfield, IN
Monday, June 8, 9:28 p.m., Lexington, Kentucky	Mark Austin	Louisville, KY
	Christian Dehner	Lexington, KY
	Mark Hawkins	Frankfort, KY
Tuesday, June 9, 1:47 a.m., Gate City, Virginia	Harold Brooks	Forest, VA
	E.L. McGuire	Bedford, VA
Tuesday, June 9, 2:05 a.m., Kingsport, Tennessee	Leon Begeman	Dale City, VA
	Harold Brooks	Forest, VA
Tuesday, June 9, 3:30 a.m., Mars Hill, North Carolina	Officer Andy Cody	Mars Hill, NC
	E.L. McGuire	Bedford, VA
Tuesday, June 9, 9:54 a.m., Greenville, South Carolina	Harold Brooks	Forest, VA
	Lisa Brown	Travelers Rest, SC
Tuesday, June 9, 11:33 a.m., Atlanta, Georgia	Gordon Frank	Dunwoody, GA
	Dave Lott	Marietta, GA
	Mike Sachs	Decatur, GA
	Steve Travis	Decatur, GA
Tuesday, June 9, 12:13 p.m., Opelika, Alabama	John Harrison	Birmingham, AL
	Bob Ray	Madison, AL
	Greg Roberts	Wadley, AL

Date, Time, Checkpoint	Witness	Home Town
Tuesday, June 9, 2:50 p.m., Century, Florida	Jim Boone	Titusville, FL
	Joel Hersch	Boca Raton, FL
	Harvey Schneider	Boca Raton, FL
	Tom Wiessner	Pensacola, FL
Tuesday, June 9, 6:28 p.m., Hattiesburg, Mississippi	Jeff Gordy	Jackson, MS
	Melinda Taylor	Hattiesburg, MS
Tuesday, June 9, 10:02 p.m., Ruston, Louisiana	Dennis Dezendorf	Natchitoches, LA
	Bill Johnson	Leesville, LA
	Dan Weber	Shreveport, LA
Wednesday, June 10, 12:10 a.m., Texarkana, Arkansas	Ken Fisher	England, AR
	Bill Freeburn	Little Rock, AR
Wednesday, June 10, 12:20 a.m., Texarkana, Texas	Randell Hendricks	Lewisville, TX
	Eddie Metz	Grapevine, TX
	Dan Vanlandingham	The Woodlands, TX
Wednesday, June 10, 1:50 a.m., Broken Bow, Oklahoma	Ardys Kellerman	Austin, TX
	Boyd Young	Atoka, OK
Wednesday, June 10, 1:25 p.m., Kansas City, Kansas	Lloyd Forester	Lenexa, KS
	Charles Purvis	Louisburg, KS
Wednesday, June 10, 1:45 p.m., Kansas City, Missouri	Paul Glaves	Lawrence, KS
	Voni Glaves	Lawrence, KS
	Scott Young	Columbia, MO
Wednesday, June 10, 5:50 p.m., Iowa City, Iowa	Pam Dempster	Iowa City, IA
	Brad Hogue	Aurora, CO
	Jeff Lambert	Rapid City, IL
	Ken Lefler	Iowa City, IA
Wednesday, June 10, 7:32 p.m., East Dubuque, Illinois	Mike Cornett	Chicago, IL
	Mike Pecora	Downers Grove, IL
	Philip Urbanek	Naperville, IL
	Todd Zedak	Chicago, IL
Wednesday, June 10, 11:15 p.m., La Crosse, Wisconsin	Jeff Dean	Madison, WI
	Debra Forbes	Muskego, WI
Thursday, June 11, 12:31 a.m., Inver Grove Heights, Minnesota	Pete Dean	Minnetonka, MN
	Joan Oswald	Bloomington, MN
	Loren Sullivan	Plano, TX
Thursday, June 11, 6:30 a.m., Fargo, North Dakota	Gary Olson	Fargo, ND
	Scott Ward	Hastings, MN
	Adam Wolkoff	St. Paul, MN

Date, Time, Checkpoint	Witness	Home Town
Thursday, June 11, 11:12 a.m., Wibaux, Montana	George Barnes DeVern Gerber Scott Ward Bill Weyher	Carbondale, CO Logan, UT Hastings, MN Salt Lake City, UT
Thursday, June 11, 12:58 p.m., Buffalo, South Dakota	DeVern Gerber Bill Weyher	Logan, UT Salt Lake City, UT
Thursday, June 11, 2:45 p.m., Sundance, Wyoming	Ren Berggren Bill Weyher	Longmont, CO Salt Lake City, UT
Thursday, June 11, 8:50 p.m., Sidney, Nebraska	Norm Babcock Linda Babcock Tony Black Tom Vervaeke	Highlands Ranch, CO Highlands Ranch, CO Colorado Springs, CO Colorado Springs, CO
Friday, June 12, 2:37 a.m., Limon, Colorado	Jeff Black Brian Boberick Brad Hogue Chris Lawson Tim Moffitt	Colorado Springs, CO Littleton, CO Aurora, CO Englewood, CO Parker, CO
Friday, June 12, 9:20 a.m., Santa Fe, New Mexico	Ira Agins David Beck Jeffery Foster Jim Hickerson	Santa Fe, NM Santa Fe, NM Albuquerque, NM Cedar Crest, NM
Friday, June 12, 3:34 p.m., Kingman, Arizona	Pablo Garcia Rob Lentini Jeff Powell Dennis Robinson	Tucson, AZ Tucson, AZ Kingman, AZ Chandler, AZ
Friday, June 12, 4:43 p.m., Needles, California	Scott Lee Jim White Pat Widder	Duarte, CA Long Beach, CA Ojai, CA
Saturday, June 13, 1:08 a.m., Ely, Nevada	Ken Carlton Warren Harhay Bill Miner Kim Rydalch	St. George, UT Boulder City, NV Sacramento, CA Modesto, CA
Saturday, June 13, 4:38 a.m., Wendover, Utah	Russell Clegg Kyle Sims Terry Smith	Salt Lake City, UT Oakland, CA Whittier, CA
Saturday, June 13, 12:48 p.m., Boise, Idaho	Michael Gasper Robert Ward Randall Weers	Kirkland, WA Bonney Lake, WA Seattle, WA

Date, Time, Checkpoint	Witness	Home Town
Saturday, June 13, 3:12 p.m., Stanfield, Oregon	Jeff Earls	Beaverton, WA
	John O'Keefe	Tigard, OR
	Bryce Ulrich	Kirkland, WA
Saturday, June 13, 3:38 p.m., Kennewick, Washington	Steve Jewett	Seattle, WA
	Tom Loftus	Port Orchard, WA
	Ron Smith	Bothell, WA
	Dale Wilson	Kennewick, WA
Sunday, June 14, 2:27 p.m., Hyder, Alaska	Herb Anderson	St. Albert, AB
	Norm Babcock	Highlands Ranch, CO
	Linda Babcock	Highlands Ranch, CO
	Chris Baldwin	Vancouver, BC
	Tracy DesLaurier	Sherwood Park, AB
	Caroline Gutierrez	Hyder, AK
	Vince Kretzul	Edmonton, AB
	Don Moses	Incline Village, NV

Appendix B

Author's 7/49 Route

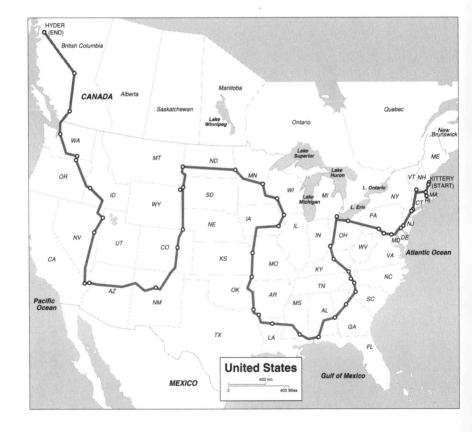

Appendix C

Fran Crane/Mike Kneebone's 48-state Route

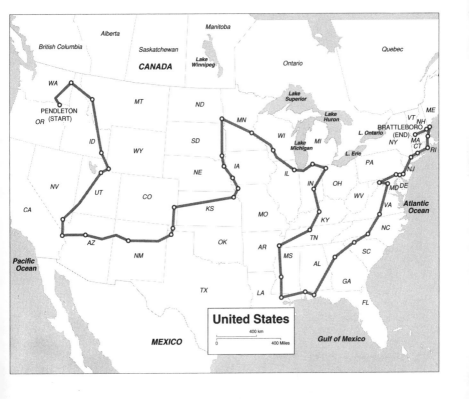

Index

About the Author

Ron Ayres is a nationally recognized motorcycle endurance rider who has completed numerous endurance competitions, including two Iron Butt rallies. His first book, *Against the Wind,* describes his participation in the 1995 Iron Butt Rally, which he finished in sixth place after riding more than 12,000 miles in eleven days. *Against the Wind* has been widely acclaimed among motorcyclists and non-riders alike and is now in its third printing.

In 1998, Ron shattered a Guinness World Record when he visited all 48 contiguous states by motorcycle in just six days. After completing his 48-state journey in Washington, he continued to Hyder, Alaska, and set a record as the first motorcyclist to visit all 49 North American states in seven days.

In 1999, Ron and his wife Barbara relocated to Johannesburg, South Africa. Ron is the Chief Executive Officer of EDS Africa, a global firm which provides information technology services to companies in sub-Saharan Africa.

Ron continues his motorcycle adventures in Africa. In March 2000, he and South African rider Shaun Powell will lead a group of experienced motorcyclists on an "8 Flags" ride through South Africa, Zimbabwe, Zambia, Botswana, Namibia, Lesotho, Swaziland, and Mozambique.

Ron maintains a web site at www.ronayres.com. His e-mail address is ron@ronayres.com.